MORE THAN BLINDFAITH

Countering the Questions of Our Culture With Clarity and Reason

JIM WALTON

THE 3RD CHOICE PUBLISHING

OTHER WORKS BY JIM WALTON

Assume Crash Position, but Enjoy the Ride:
The Diary of A Middle School Parent
The 3rd Choice Publishing, 2016

Six Rivers: Dominant Themes Watering the Biblical Landscape
The 3rd Choice Publishing, 2016

Growing A Youth Ministry
The 3rd Choice Publishing, 2016

To my wife, Denise More Loizeaux Walton
who has been so patient with me all these years
through all my various projects,
hobbies, and interests.
"I love you today."
- JW

ABOUT THE AUTHOR

Jim Walton is a career youth pastor, having served on church staff in that capacity for 35 years. In addition to youth pastor, as is common on church staffs he also served as Director of Christian Education, Choir Director, Assistant Pastor, interim pastor, Worship Leader, and Pastor of Family Ministries.

Jim got his B.A. degree (with honors) in Christian Education from Wheaton College, and an M.A. (with honors) in Christian Ministry from Wheaton Graduate School. He has written four books, has been published dozens of times in magazines and journals, and has given seminars at the national level (Youth Specialties National Youth Workers Convention), at colleges (Houghton College, Cairn University), many New York State Sunday School Conventions, Iron Sharpens Iron Men's Conferences, churches, events, and he participates in discussion forums. He has spoken at more than 100 retreats, has led both domestic and foreign missions trips, and has trained pastors in other countries.

He is currently the founder and director of "The 3rd Choice," an evangelistic, apologetics, and discipling online ministry—reclaiming people with the truth of Christ.

CONTENTS

INTRODUCTION

There is such a thing as truth, and it can be known. I am a purveyor of that truth. My ministry is The 3rd Choice, and I consider myself to be an apologist (giving evidence that what Christians believe is reasonable), an evangelist, and a discipler. I believe Christianity is true, and have written this book to show why.

Cynics and skeptics are quick to accuse how presumptuous it is of me to claim I have a corner on the truth when the world is so busy searching for answers, and there are so many answers in play. Many lose faith and claim that the truth can never be known amidst all the choices, while others conclude that there are so many truths they must all be valid. Either way, our hands are empty.

These are both positions of despair, and they paint us into a false corner—a round corner that isn't really there, and the challengers think they can keep turning us in circles. Yet truth can be known, and the true seekers of this world, directed by the Holy Spirit, are able to find it and know it. It's a genuine treasure that can be defined, explained, and shared.

I'm not the only one with access to the truth. There are actually billions of us. My vision, or task, is to use the Internet and social media to engage people in conversation about the truth and logic of God, the reliability of the Bible, the treasure that is Jesus Christ and his salvation, and to engage people in dialogue on any spiritual subject. Christians have a rational and reasonable belief in God and His Word that makes sense out of our lives and the world.

I believe, ultimately, that truth is not merely a philosophical proposition or a mere coincidence of hypothesis with reality. I believe that truth is ultimately a person—the person of Jesus Christ. As such, truth is objective, personal, moral, and has a perfect correspondence with reality. Jesus can articulate true philosophical and theological propositions as well as show us how life really works, how it's supposed to work, and its true points of interaction between spiritual and physical life. It is this truth that shines like light in the world. As an apologist, my task is to break down barriers so that it—He—can be seen, and to give evidence that the Christian faith is indeed reasonable.

PREFACE

Our culture is presently engaged in a great tug of war over truth. For millennia, religious ideas towered over the landscape as much as church steeples dominated the skylines of towns. While Christian tenets were often disregarded, culture was still grounded on the foundation of Christianity, and people lived on borrowed principles. Yet new information has created new doubts. In the present age, education and science have opened new conversations. Archaeology has come into its own, and the earth itself has brought forth a new voice: the artifacts of ages past are telling us information that has been buried for thousands of years, and this data is changing the perspectives of our culture. For many, confidence has been replaced by confusion.

The scientific community continues to reach farther into space, deeper into microbiology, mysteriously into quantum mechanics, and boldly into genetic research. The results have been striking, spectacular, and awe-inspiring. Our new knowledge is so breathtaking that it has motivated some to declare that all old knowledge, including anything religious, is now not only suspect, but able to be discarded., as if the borrowed principles are no longer valid. "We know better now. We have science."

For some, science has become the new religion, regarded as the source and bastion of all truth, the discipline that holds the answers or potential answers to all questions. Science is to be believed even where evidence or direct proofs are lacking, knowing that "someday we'll learn these things," just as in the days of Copernicus, Galileo, and Einstein. Eventually all will be known, and science will be the angel of light. Issues that were formerly left to other disciplines, such as...

- Why are we here?
- Why does anything exist?
- Is there a God?
- Is there purpose in life?
- What makes something right or wrong?
- What is love?
- What are thoughts, and reason?

...are all projected to be within the realm of science. But does science legitimately have this kind of reach? Is it valid that theistic ideas are doomed to an eventual death at the hand of science, or at least relegated to a distant cave where primitive and ignorant people still cling to worthless ideas of God (the Flying Spaghetti Monster, a pink unicorn), religious purpose, and the "silliness" of objective morality?

I'm quite convinced that is not and will never be the case. Christians have no basis to shrink back in fear, for in the tug of war for truth, our end is tied to a Rock and will not be moved. While science and archaeology have many legitimate points to which we need to give high regard, to treat with respect, and to incorporate into our knowledge base of "things that are so," science is claiming more than science can ever rightly know. Science is not the core and end of all knowledge. Ultimately, objective truth is an anchor that stands behind religious, theistic, biblical, Christian thought, as well as behind science. In that we can have firm confidence—the non-negotiable and firm substantiation that what we've been taught from the Bible is really true, and we can be absolutely certain of some things even if we can't measure them by scientific means or prove them in a laboratory.

CHAPTER 1
THE EXISTENCE OF GOD

Before we can discuss what God—a supreme supernatural divine being—is like, what his nature is, and how he acts, any discussion of life and religion has to do determine whether or not such a being exists. If God doesn't exist, there's no point in talking about whether He allows evil, if He is good or cruel, what it means that He's all-powerful and all-knowing, or the possibility of miracles. Until we establish that it is rational to believe that there is a God, we can't even leave the starting blocks. The race is over before it begins.

I took an informal survey of pastors on the "Pastor Network" on LinkedIn, asking them, "How do you know there's a God?" Their answers clustered around several themes:

- Design in creation
- Miraculous healings
- The Holy Spirit speaking to me
- The Holy Scriptures speaking to me
- Fulfilled prophecy
- The existence of the nation of Israel
- Personal experience

I also took an informal survey of atheists on reddit.com, asking them, "How do you know there is no God?" Their answers were as follows:

- There is no actual evidence for God, and so there's no reason to believe there is one. God is no different from Hobbits: completely fictional. There is no discernible difference between god(s) and anything else made up by people.
- I have a strong intuition that the thought of God makes it really difficult to accept that it's true.
- Yahweh is logically self-refuting.
- Occam's Razor (which says the simplest explanation is the best explanation). If my army wins a battle, it's simpler to assume there was some strategic advantage or circumstantial luck than think a divine being intervened. In other words, unless direct evidence forces you in another direction, the simplest explanation should be taken as the most likely explanation.
- I've never been given convincing reasons to believe that a god exists.

The reader can readily detect a wide divergence of perspective. Is He there, or isn't He? Did I get better because I healed, or because there was divine intervention? Was that God talking to me, or was it my own thought? Questioning God's existence is a common human query. When we pray and nothing happens, we wonder. When there is tragedy in our lives, we wonder. When there doesn't seem to be any divine justice on earth, we wonder. Most of us never hear voices; we don't see visions. There are many religions on the earth, and always have been. Is there one God? Are there many? What is this divine being like, and how can I know? None of us wants to be stupid, believing in fantasies and magic, and talking to thin air. Yet if God really exists, it changes all of life. It's a question that enters everyone's mind at some point in his or her life.

Are there any evidences for God—real evidences, and if so, what are they? First I wish to say that when the debate gets truthful and real, no one can *prove* there is a God, nor can anyone *prove* there isn't one. We must go for the most reasonable conclusion, not for undeniable proof. In the movie "Zero Dark Thirty," about the assassination of Osama bin Laden, the C.I.A. Director asks if it is certain that bin Laden is in the suspected location or not. The answer comes back, "We don't deal in certainty, we deal in probability." It is possible to know truth without proof. Empirical proof is not always the final court of appeals. The wise course is to weigh the claims and infer the conclusion that makes the most sense. Given what we see and know, and examining the evidences and weighing the logic, does belief in God make more sense than believing that there is no God?

We can start off by drawing an enormous imaginary circle that represents all the knowledge of humanity. Inside the circle we'll put archaeology, astronomy, anthropology, anatomy, architecture, biology, chemistry, geology, mathematics, physics, philosophy, paleontology, psychology, political science, economics, engineering, theology, history, languages, sociology, social work, zoology, and a thousand other things—all the composite knowledge of humankind. Now inside that prodigious circle draw a circle that represents how much of all that you personally know. I'm confident that any of us who are honest would be hard pressed to make a dot small enough. The bottom line is that we each have to admit how little we know. Given that reality, can people actually say with confidence that there is no God? Very few will; most who deny the existence of God will say that the evidence just isn't strong enough.

There are, however, plenty of strong submissions for the existence of God. But before we get to that we have to talk a little about metaphysics: the existence of being. "Why is there something rather than nothing?" mused existentialist philosopher Jean-Paul Sartre. We're here, and the universe is here. Why is that?

While any philosopher worth his salt can argue any of us under the table about how we can't logically prove that *anything* exists, most of us assume there really is a physical world, that matter and energy are real, and our reasoning ability is reliable enough to comprehend the world we see around us and organize our thoughts to make sense out of it. Science, along with all of our academic disciplines, would be meaningless if this were not the case.

But in the recognition of the things that exist, it is also obvious that there are different kinds of existence. Time exists in a completely different way than the chair in which I am sitting. My memories are a different fabric than my shirt. The truths of math exist in a different sense than the truths of biology. Some existences are material while others are not; some existences are concrete while others are abstract. My thoughts are just as real as the TV set, but in a completely different way. Those metaphysical realizations pave the way for our discussion about the possible existence of God.

THE QUESTION OF KNOWLEDGE: HOW DO WE KNOW WHAT WE KNOW?

Knowledge is a tricky business. How do you know you know what you know? And how would you know if you knew it? Can you be sure you're not dreaming or hallucinating? Can you be sure you're perceiving things correctly? How do you even know you're awake? We've seen enough science fiction movies to know how dicey things like this can get. Maybe you've been injected with a drug that makes you *think* you're experiencing what you are ("Total Recall"), or a great computer is creating the world you imagine you perceive ("The Matrix"). Maybe it's all a dream ("Inception")? There's even the contrived world of "The Truman Show". Well, how do you know? Again, if you talk with a philosopher, he or she can prove to you how uncertain all of knowledge really is. The conversation can get you going in so many circles that you don't know which way is up any more, and even if you knew it, you couldn't really be sure of it.

The field of the study of knowledge is called epistemology. Practically speaking, at the end of the day, my epistemic conclusions (what I know and how I know it) have to contain at least some things that I assume to be true, because many things simply cannot be proved.

- I assume that external physical objects are materially real, and have an objective existence outside of my sensory experience of them. In other words, things really exist whether I experience them or not and whether or not I even perceive them accurately. They have an objective existence outside of my mind, body, and experience.
- I assume, because I have experienced it, that sometimes my senses can deceive me, so that the truth of something or the truth about something doesn't depend on me or my experiences.
- I assume that some truths don't have a sensory component to

them, such as the abstract truths of mathematics. Things can be true even though they can't be touched, seen, heard, tasted, or smelled.

- I assume that though my senses can deceive me, I can consider them reliable when they coincide with the reality of existing objective physical objects.

In a sense it seems unnecessary to have to say these things, but my point is that when it comes to knowledge, the things I claim to know, at bottom, are based on my assumptions about what the world is like and how it works, what my senses and experiences tell me, especially compared and contrasted with the senses and experiences of others. These things I assume are called my presuppositions.

Even in the best of situations, we base our knowledge on certain things we *believe*. "We know what we know" because we make assumptions about what is knowable. We hardly think about it, but we even have beliefs about whether our assumptions dictate what we believe, or whether we believe that our experiences dictate what our assumptions will be. So much of what we know comes off the foundation of our presuppositions, and basically what we choose to believe about what we know.

I don't think it's evasive to come to a point where we choose to insert the subjective notion of "common sense" to make sense of knowledge. It's a bit circular, because I have to make assumptions about what I know so that I know what I assume, and I have to make assumptions about what I believe that feeds into what I believe I know. Knowledge certainly has to accord with objective reality, usually what we as people agree about, but we also admit that knowledge is possible through abstract reasoning disengaged from sensory experiences. Therefore truth exists outside of myself (there is such a thing as reality that is not subject to my experience of it). Knowledge is based on belief as well as evidence, for ultimately I choose which evidences to believe that become what I consider knowledge.

Why am I bothering with all this? Because it all pertains to how we know God exists.

THE QUESTION OF LOGIC: ARGUMENTS FOR THE EXISTENCE OF GOD

Some people claim to have experienced God, even to have seen Him or heard Him. Others claim that there is not and never has been any objective evidence that a supreme divine being exists. If we cannot rely on the consistency of the empirical (what we know through experience or experiment) evidence for God, then our first challenge is to reason His existence. There are set "proofs" of the existence of God that have been presented through the ages. The intent behind them is that they affirm that belief in a supreme divine being is reasonable.

The first set of arguments about God's existence are called cosmological arguments, which means they pertain to origins (Why is there something rather than nothing? How did what we see get here?) and to cause and effect (What caused what we see to exist?).

The Cosmological Argument

The cosmological arguments claim that everything we see around us had to have come from somewhere, something that made it come into existence. Things don't just pop into existence all by themselves. Other things make them come into existence.

Ilm al-Kalam proposed that unless there was a beginning, there wouldn't be a present. Think of it this way: Suppose you go to the grocery store and, approaching the deli counter, you plan to take a ticket for your proper turn. But on the ticket-dispenser, you see a sign that says, "Before taking this ticket, you must take a ticket from the machine on the right." You reach for that machine, but it also has a similar sign on it. The third machine has the same sign. And the fourth. This could go on forever (which is Kalam's point), unless you finally get to a machine somewhere in the line that allows you to take a ticket. Unless there is a beginning, there can be no present.

What he is arguing is that somewhere there must be a First Cause, something (or Someone) that was always there to kick the whole thing into gear, to cause everything else. The cosmological argument states that God is a reasonable possibility as the First Cause.

Scientists are on the hunt for "the beginning." They use mathematics to extrapolate back to "the beginning." Using the observable expanding universe as factors in the equation, the theory holds that way back in time, before the Bang, there existed only an infinitesimally small point of no dimension and no matter, where the laws of physics as we know them were not in operation. If that is the case, so goes the cosmological argument, a supreme, supernatural divine being outside of what we know as nature is a logical candidate to be the First Cause.

What explains the beginning? Since such realities cannot be observed with our senses or tested in a lab, and since the laws of physics and the forces of the universe were not operational, theists claim that no explanation for the universe can be found from nature's own existence —the mechanism that caused the universe was external to itself. While alternatives for what that mechanism was are continually theorized and discussed, God is not an irrational choice among the options.

Here is the way Kalam's argument looks:

1. Everything that begins to exist has a cause.
2. The universe began to exist.
3. Therefore, the universe has a cause.

We know of nothing that began at one time to exist spontaneously of its own volition—nothing that we know of is self-caused. We know of nothing that at any time began to exist from its own nature (How can something pop itself into existence when it doesn't exist?). Everything that *had* a beginning was brought into existence by something else that already existed, whether technological, mechanical, or even biological. Even biological things came from other biological things, or at least from something that already existed. Something had to always have existed. So what caused the universe to begin to exist? It has to have had a cause. God is a reasonable choice as to that cause.

In addition to the cosmological arguments, there are cases that can be made for the existence of God coming from other angles.

The Ontological Argument

Ontology means the nature of being or the nature of existence—how it is that things exist. This piece of reasoning comes from Alvin Plantinga.[1] He argues that God is a necessary being.

1. If God (a supreme, supernatural divine being) does not exist, his existence is logically impossible. That doesn't mean he can't be made up in someone's imagination (which is still possible even if he doesn't exist); what it means is that if God doesn't really exist, the very concept of God is inconsistent or self-contradictory. His existence doesn't even make sense.

2. But if God *does* exist, then it's necessary that He does. It cannot be otherwise if He is truly God and if He truly exists.
3. Therefore (first conclusion), God's existence is either impossible (inconsistent and self-contradictory) or necessary. There's no half-way position.
4. If God's existence is logically impossible, then even the concept of God and everything we think about him is contradictory. We are trying to make a reality what is not only nonsensical, but impossible.
5. But the concept of God is not contradictory. There's actually good sense to it in many ways, for example, that something caused what we see. While some may not agree, it's assuredly not contradictory.
6. Therefore (second conclusion), if God's existence isn't contradictory (if that choice is removed from the equation), then the only reasonable choice left is that God is logically necessary.

God is either impossible or necessary. Since He's not impossible, then He must be necessary, and therefore He exists.

---

[1] Alvin Plantinga, <u>God and Other Minds: a Study of the Rational Justification of Belief in God</u>, (Ithaca, NY: Cornell University Press, 1967), p. 83

The Teleological Argument

Teleology pertains to purpose. We as humans assume teleology. When we see something, we innately ask, "Why?" We assume there's a purpose behind it, a reason for what we see. We forever catch ourselves thinking, "I wonder why it did that?" or "Why did that happen?" We assume purpose—that things happen for a reason. If we apply this argument to the existence of God, we end up with an argument such as this:

1. We as humans don't know of anything that shows evidence of being purposefully designed that wasn't indeed purposefully designed. Whenever we know of something that exhibits purpose (a reason for why it exists or why something happened the way it did), and whenever we know whether or not it was the product of intelligent design (somebody thought it up and made it happen), it was indeed the designed product of an intelligent being. Whether a watch, a washer, or a window, if we can infer that there was a purpose behind it, it's safe to say that an intelligent being designed it for that purpose, or at least for *a* purpose.
2. There are many parts of the universe, the earth, and life as we know it that exhibit purpose—not just parts of the universe exhibit purpose, though, but even the universe itself. Every scientist asks "Why?" We assume purpose in what we observe around us. "Why do the planets spin?" "Why is the earth pitched at an angle?" We are always looking for the reasons and the purpose, assuming they are there and, not surprisingly, we find purpose in many parts of the universe and life.
3. Therefore, it's logical to assume that the universe could be the product of purposeful design.
4. Everything else we know that exhibits those characteristics was indeed designed; why should the universe be treated any differently?

Purpose doesn't logically sprout all by itself. We invest things with purpose, give them purpose, and design them with purpose.

When archaeologists dig something up, they can see that it was made, and they ask, "Hm, what was this for? What purpose did it have?" The universe has similar characteristics that are means to ends—cause and effect for a purpose. It's logical, then, based on everything else we know, to assume a designer when we see a design. That's the rationale behind the teleological argument.

The Analogical Argument

An analogy is using one common and understandable thing to help us understand another thing. This argument is similar to the teleological argument of design, and it uses an analogy (hence analogical). It also comes from Alvin Plantinga.[2]

1. Everything that we as humans produce for a particular purpose is designed for that purpose by someone intelligent enough to have designed it.
2. The universe is like that in that it has many characteristics that seem like it was produced for a particular purpose.

3. Therefore it makes sense that the universe could have been designed for the purpose it fulfills by someone intelligent enough to have designed it.
4. Therefore whoever designed the universe is a being intelligent enough to have designed everything we see.

The Existence of Other Minds Besides Our Own (also from Plantinga):

There's a double argument from both purpose and by analogy, reasoning that we can infer the existence of God in the same way that we "know" the existence of other persons. We know that we are not alone in the world because we know there are other persons in it. We also believe that each one has a mind that can reason, feel, remember, intuit, etc., just as ours can. Yet I have absolutely no concrete evidence of anyone else's mind. I can never really tell if they think, what they

[2] Ibid. pp. 96-97

are truly feeling, if their pain is real and what it is like, etc., and yet I suppose it's true. I can never determine by observation that someone else is in a particular mental state. But I can reasonably construct a sound inductive argument for the conclusion that I am not the only being that thinks and reasons, or has sensations and feelings. How do we know that other people think, similar to the way I think, and feel things similar to what I feel? When it comes right down to it, other minds are inaccessible to me, and their attributes are similarly inaccessible. I have no observational proof of them. And yet we live life fully convinced that there are other people, that they have thoughts and feelings, and that our perceptions and analyses of such things are both reasonable and to varying extents accurate.

I can't scientifically prove to you what another person is thinking, or even that they are thinking, or if they are feeling pain. And yet there are cues, clues, and evidences that tell me such things. Scientific evidences ultimately fail in this regard. With so many variables, what the analogy holds here is that *for any person there are direct arguments for the propositions in question, and given that there is no comparable evidence against them, they must be more probable than not on his total evidence.* The bulk of my commonsense beliefs about minds and mental states must be more probable than not on my total evidence. I have evidence that other sentient beings exist, but that's not enough to confirm that they experience anger, joy, depression, and pain, as well as hold beliefs. It's neither necessary nor possible that I am able to observe such entities to be able to assume truth.

Using the analogy, then, belief in God is rational, being more probable than not on the total evidence.

Continuing the thought, the universe exhibits many characteristics of design, though I can't prove design in the science lab. There are many elements of apparent design in the universe.

1. The rate of expansion of the universe. If any more or less, the universe would not be suited for life as we know it.
2. The ratio of the electromagnetic force to gravity must be one part to 10^{40}. Anything else would not sustain life.

3. DNA contains information, and information (as far as we know) can only come from an informational source.[3]
4. The irreducible complexity of the bacterial flagellum[4]
5. The human eye[5]
6. The strong and weak nuclear force exist in an extremely narrow band of effectiveness

If everything we know of that works like it was designed for a purpose was indeed designed for a purpose, and the universe has elements suggesting it was designed for a purpose, then it logically could easily have been designed by an intelligence big enough to handle the task. That's using the evidence we have to infer a reasonable conclusion. That reasonable conclusion would be the existence of God.

Similar to that is Moreland's argument from consciousness:[6]

1. Genuinely nonphysical mental states exist (feelings, thoughts, emotions). (If you deny the existence of mental states, all discourse becomes unintelligible and absurd.)
2. The explanation for the existence of mental states is either personal or scientific. Personal explanation is different from natural scientific explanation. Personal explanations intend to account for specific events or results by appealing to a free, moral agent.
3. The explanation for nonphysical mental states is not a natural scientific one, for no naturalistic explanation postulated thus far has been capable of accounting for how the mental can arise from the physical.
   a. The uniformity of nature: no amount of restructuring of the primal physical stuff of the universe can produce something as distinct as mental states.
   b. The contingency of the mind-body correlation: there seems to be no inherent and necessary connection

---

[3] William Dembski

[4] William Paley

[5] Michael Behe

[6] J.P. Moreland, Consciousness and the Existence of God: A Theistic Argument (New York, NY: Routledge, 2008)

between the mental states to the physical states on which they depend.

 c. The causal closure of physical states. If physical events have only physical causes, how is it that we have thoughts? Yet if our thoughts can create physical changes as well as mental changes, this implies mental events are separate from physical events.

 d. Evolutionary explanations are inadequate, because consciousness is not necessary to survival, as any tree will tell you.

4. Therefore, the explanation for nonphysical mental states is a personal one.

5. If the explanation is personal, then it is theistic (a free, moral agent outside of the physical), best explained by the existence of a supreme, supernatural divine being.

The Axiological Argument

"Axios" is a Greek work meaning "honor; worth; value." The axiological argument is about morals and morality. This argument comes from Ravi Zacharias.[7]

1. It is commonly admitted that there is evil in the world. People believe that some things are just wrong.

2. But if evil exists, one must also assume that good also exists in order to know the difference.

3. And if good and evil exist, one must assume that some kind of standard exists to measure what is good and what is evil. Again, people commonly believe that there are standards of right and wrong, good and bad. That would lead us to believe that a moral law exists that allows us to evaluate such things.

4. If a moral law exists, then that moral law has a source. Where did the moral law come from—our "standard" of what is right and what is wrong? It must have come from somewhere, or there must at least be an objective basis for it.

---

[7] Ravi Zacharias, Jesus Among Others Gods: The Absolute Claims of the Christian Message, (Nashville, TN: Thomas Nelson Publishers, 2000), p. 112

5. It makes sense that the source of our personal, objective moral law must also be personal, moral, and objective.
6. Therefore God—a personal, moral source outside of humanity—must exist.

In addition, I also find evidence for the existence of God in the following:

1. Order in nature. Theism is a far more logical causal mechanism for the order we see than the random processes of natural selection.
2. Extrapolations backwards based on theories and agendas are, frankly, outside of the scope of true science. The universe exhibits an order, complexity, and balance beyond the parameters possible in a system governed by pure chance. The picture the Bible gives is that God is a God of order; evolution talks about random development. Order, then, is more theistically-oriented than atheistic.
3. Purpose in nature. While science (inductive reasoning) and my five senses can tell me what is there and how it works, it cannot explain the area of purpose that observations reveal to be universal to humanity. We all have a sense of purpose, a desire for purpose, and a quest for meaning that is evidence of a foundation in the universe consistent with the existence of a divine being, and inconsistent with the limitations of a closed system of random coincidences regulated by natural processes.
4. Consistency in nature. Astronomers can tell us the solar and lunar eclipses for multi-millennia in both directions, past and future. We can do the math so that we can blast off a rocket from earth and have it reach the moon in the way and time desired. Physical constants (electromagnetic, atomic and nuclear, physico-chemical, gravitational, etc.) not only make our world livable but they make science possible. If we were to weigh the likelihood that these aspects of life came from an intelligent source or from random processes, it's not at all unreasonable to conclude that the intelligent source makes

more sense (unless one presupposes that God is impossible—but the evidence leads us more rationally to an intelligent source than an accidental one).

FIRST CONCLUSION

What I have done is laid out seven arguments showing it is both logical and reasonable to believe in God. Don't make the mistake, however, of thinking that these arguments are watertight and impregnable to attack. We all know that a refutation can be made against any argument. No matter what evidence one produces it's always possible to find someone who will disagree. I know I haven't proved God, but I never claimed I could or would. My design, or purpose (teleology) is to show that believing in the existence of God makes a lot of sense and is possibly the simplest explanation (Occam's Razor) for the phenomena we see. What I'm trying to do is reason to the best inference, given the reality we know. What we see around us is:

- A universe that had a beginning
- A universe and life forms that appear designed
- A universe that exhibits purpose, order, regularity, and predictability
- The existence of nonphysical mental states, and the observance of the same in other people
- A standard behind societies of right and wrong: objective moral truths

Therefore belief in God was, and still is, a reasonable conclusion by thinking people. It's a position that can be logically postulated and reasonably defended.

THE NATURE AND DEFINITION OF FAITH

I believe knowledge is what we've learned, understand, and remember from the past and present, and faith is our expectation of what will happen in the immediate and far future based on what we've learned from the past. In other words, and maybe more clearly, faith isn't a leap in the dark; faith is not "believing something unreasonable with all your heart," as has been accused. Faith is always an assumption of truth based on enough evidence to make it reasonable for you to make that assumption. Let me explain.

When you sit down in a chair, you don't think twice about sitting down. You have enough faith that the chair will hold you. Faith? Yes. You've sat in chairs hundreds of times, but you can never be absolutely sure it will hold you this time. Chairs do break on occasion. But you make an assumption of truth based on enough evidence to make it reasonable for you to make that assumption, and you sit down. It's an act of faith, and it has nothing to do with a leap in the dark. It has to do with knowledge and evidence, but because the result is unknown and unknowable until you act, it's an act of faith.

Almost all of life is by faith because we can never know what lies ahead. Every time you turn a doorknob you are expressing faith. Possibly 10,000 times you've turned a doorknob, and it opened the door, so you turn the knob and move forward. Does it always work that way? No. Sometimes you turn the knob and the door doesn't open. But you make an assumption of truth based on enough evidence to make it reasonable for you to make that assumption.

We know chairs hold people. That's past experience and learning. We know turning doorknobs opens doors. We know when we turn a key or push a button a car starts. That's all knowledge. But every time we turn a car key, it's an exercise of faith. We don't know for sure the car will start, and unfortunately sometimes it doesn't. Then we use our knowledge to try to figure out what to do about it. We dial our phone (as an act of faith, assuming it will work and help us reach another person) and try to get help.

It becomes clear we live our lives by faith—all of us, every day, every action, because we can't know anything future. Yet we assume what will happen based on the evidence and our experience.

Faith doesn't just apply to the unknown future, though, it is also assurance of what has happened in the past (cf. Hebrews 11:3). Applying tests of reality, trust in the consistency and reason in the pieces of historical record we have, combined with confidence in the existence of God and His activity in the world, we can also form a knowledge of past events with relative confidence.

Therefore, my faith in God, or in the existence of God, is not a blind leap in the dark. It is an assumption of truth based on enough evidence to make it reasonable for me to make that assumption. In the Bible, God revealed himself to Abraham before Abraham was expected to have faith in Him. He appeared to Moses in a burning bush and spoke to Him, confirming his power with miracles before Moses was expected to believe. He sent Moses back to the Egyptian leaders and the Israelite people with wonders to reveal who He was before He expected faith. Based on the objective, empirical evidence, faith was to issue forth as a response.

At some point we add reason to observation to come to a conclusion that makes it reasonable to make an assumption of truth. Did Alexander the Great exist? We have no eyewitnesses who are still alive, and he cannot be proved by our five senses. But we place credibility in the historical documents that point to his existence and we observe the changes that have come to the world through Hellenistic influences, and so we believe it even though we can't see it. In a sense, you can't *know* God exists anymore than you can *know* the American Civil War happened. But since we claim to know that the Civil War happened, it's also reasonable to claim that I know God exists. You choose to believe the evidences that give credence and credibility to the historicity of the conflict, and you accept it as truth. It's no different from my belief in God that I consider to be based on reasonable recognitions of credibility, veracity, documentation, and observation. At its core, then, all (or almost all) of knowledge is really faith, since I'm choosing to believe which sources I will consider reliable, and therefore everything I "know" is really that I'm choosing to trust those sources of information, be they my teachers, textbooks, various historical documents, or whatever.

Good faith, like good science, needs sound, rational thinking. Christianity is based in presuppositions combined with evidences, not in blind beliefs. Hebrews 11.1 confirms it. "Now faith is being sure of what we hope for and certain of what we do not see." There's no blind leap here. The word for "being sure of" is ὑπόστασις (*hupostasis*). It is defined as "assurance; what stands under anything (a building, a contract, a promise); substantial nature; essence, actual being; reality (often in contrast to what merely seems to be); confidence; conviction; steadfastness; steadiness of mind." "The steadfastness of mind which holds one firm." The term is common in ancient business documents as the basis or guarantee of transactions. There's nothing wobbly or blind here. It's not just confidence, but a guarantee. It's a real knowledge, though (like the chair, the doorknob, and the car key) I can only stand on evidence, reason, and knowledge about things that haven't happened yet. But I can make an assumption of truth about God and my Christian belief based on enough evidence to make it reasonable to make that assumption. And again, what we're talking about is inferring the most reasonable conclusion.

The verse also says we can be sure of what we hope for (what is still future). Faith is more than optimism, and it's more than wishful thinking. Faith is knowledge, pure and simple. But faith understands there are different kinds of knowledge. Some knowledge is because of what I've already experienced (I know I had Cheerios™ for breakfast), and yet other knowledge is because of evidence, even though I haven't seen (my getting in the car and heading to the store, "knowing" it is there).

Hebrews 11.1 continues: "…and certain of what we do not see." The word for "certain of" is ἔλεγχος (*elegchos*). It means "proof; proving; conviction; being sure of." At what point did people get the idea that Christian faith is "intellectually dishonest," "willful ignorance," or that "faith is blind," all accusations I have heard? The faith of the Bible is distinctly evidentiary and based in knowledge. God never asked anyone to believe in him without first giving some kind of evidence. Whether it is Abraham, Moses, David, Daniel, Jesus, Paul, or anyone else in the Bible, evidence precedes faith. God spoke to Abraham, appeared to Moses in a burning bush, performed miracles for Pharaoh, strengthened David in the killing of Goliath, and on and on. Jesus performed miracles, taught, and healed people before he ever asked that people believe in him.

THE QUESTION OF SCIENCE

The scientific advancements of our culture are absolutely staggering. From the Scientific Revolution to the Age of Enlightenment, through the Industrial Revolution to the Technological Revolution, humanity through science has fueled inquiry and capability beyond anyone's wildest dreams. Can you imagine someone from the American Civil War era being brought into our culture? What the past 150 years has brought forth is nothing less than illustrious. Science has become the dominating force in our culture for knowledge, almost to a fault. But what has risen recently is the thought that science is *everything*, that it encompasses all knowledge and all possible knowledge, and if something can't be handled, examined, and evaluated by scientific means, it is suspect both as knowledge and as truth. While science has taken humankind to breathtaking heights, this claim breaks the beaker.

In refutation, there are many disciplines—legitimate limbs of learning—that repeatable, predictable, and observable strategies based on inductive reasoning don't touch. For example, economics, history, politics, poetry, theater, psychology, philosophy, theology, jurisprudence (the theory or philosophy of law), and music all fit the bill quite well. Some people exalt science to the position of "the god of our culture," making all the decisions on values, morals, truth, origins, destinies, purpose, and meaning, but such things are beyond its reach.

Scientific philosophers and epistemologists have called science to the table many times to define accurately what is science and what is not, and how scientists can know that what they know is reliable knowledge. As you might expect from my previous paragraphs, knowledge is not as rock-solid as people claim, even scientific knowledge. It turns out that more is based on assumptions and beliefs than one might imagine. Through various academic strolls through logical positivism, falsificationism, logical empiricism, under-determination, and the sociology of science, some extremists have even concluded that the totality of our so-called knowledge or beliefs is a man-made fabric that impinges on experience only along the edges,[8] or that in the end, science seems to be little more than opinion, expert opinion granted, but still just an opinion.[9] I'll grant that's extreme, but it's interesting that these ideas circulate in the public forum.

Attorney W. Mark Lanier, in his book *Christianity On Trial*[10] says it well when he says that science is not the appropriate laboratory for testing faith. He says there are many valid units of measurement: gallons, inches, kilograms, degrees Fahrenheit, etc. We would never say the temperature is six gallons, or that I put twelve Fahrenheit in my car's gas tank. Each category works to measure its own category, but not matters outside its category. We must use the right measuring system for the category or item being measured.

In the same way, Lanier says, "we err in any discussion of the existence of God if we use the wrong measure of proof. It is as absurd to think of proving God in the scientific sense of a lab process or the mathematical precision of a calculator as it is to measure distance by gallons. Ultimate questions like God's existence call for an appropriate measurement of proof."[11]

He uses the example of a courtroom. While scientists are often called to the witness stand to testify and to give expert opinion about matters of interest in the case, the scientists (and not even the science) do not pronounce the verdict. It's not the most appropriate measure of innocence or guilt. A group of reasoned minds—the people of the jury, give consideration to the science, but also to the extenuating circumstances, motives, personalities, environment, and social context in making their decision. Science is but one avenue of knowledge, and sometimes not even the most important one.

God is only observable as he acts in our world, which of course is not subject to prediction, control groups, and reproducibility. Yet there are ways to know God outside of observation. We can speak of the evidences of God in logical terms (cosmological, teleological, etc.), historical terms (the revelation of Scripture and the testimony of

---

[8] Ian Hutchinson, Monopolizing Knowledge, (Belmont, MA: Fias Publishing, 2011), p. 86

[9] Ibid. p. 88

[10] W. Mark Lanier, Christianity on Trial, (Downers Grove, IL: IVP Books, 2014)

[11] Ibid. p. 35

history, the existence of the Jewish nation, etc.), experiential terms (the evidences for God that we see in our lives and in the lives of others), as well as the design, order and purpose of nature, the delicate balance and precise parameters of the universe that make life possible, realities such as morality, justice, peace, and conscience, and aesthetics such as beauty—these are the appropriate measurements of proof of the existence of God.

THE iPOD ANALOGY

Let's just suppose, for the sake of analogy, that I have an iPod that has only one mechanism: shuffle. I get great songs one after another, but can I reasonably expect that some day the iPod will give me a sequence of my favorite songs, of all metal music, Beethoven's symphonies in order, or an awesome playlist? Yes, it might happen accidently one day, but I really can't *expect* it to happen. If it happens it would be an accident, because the only element in the system is "shuffle". How long will it take the iPod to figure out what I like and select it for me? Never. Something mechanistic has no hope of developing consciousness, and "intent" will never be an outcome of a sequence of songs. The sequence will never have meaning, and even if it did accidentally, the machine would be incapable of learning from that and selecting it again, or at least doing a better job next time around.

Evolutionary Naturalism claims that the universe we know came from random processes (the universe on "shuffle"), but that in the process it (we) learned consciousness, developed reason, evolved purposes, and became well suited for life. My contrasting contention is that this is not as reasonable a belief system (and it is a belief system) as the conclusion that personality came from a personal source, information came from an intelligent source, purpose stemmed from design, and the order and regularity of laws and forces came from a plan.

Can I confirm for you with certainty that God exists? No, I cannot. How do I know God exists? I've given you multiple appropriate logical ways. Does it *prove* the existence of God? Of course not, but it does speak loudly that God is the most reasonable answer to the situation of our existence and the world as we see it. If it is our responsibility to infer the most reasonable conclusion, not proving a matter but giving evidence beyond a reasonable doubt, a supreme divine being fits the bill.

God has given us convincing evidence in many different arenas, accessible from various vantage points, by true presuppositions, logic, the weight of evidence, my own experience, and understanding the place of faith. I can claim on that foundation with confidence and assurance that I can know God exists.

Ian Hutchinson says the same point is true in the scientific world. Speaking of science and the sociology of science, he concludes that, lacking an agreed-upon definition of science by scientists, they are not bothered by the lack of epistemic proof of what they know. "Scientists themselves are generally of the opinion that they know science without difficulty when they see it."[11] Thomas Kuhn concurs and says there is "no standard higher than the consent of the relevant community": a situation that has been colorfully characterized as scientific mob rule.[12] If that's so in science, there's no reason to criticize the same pattern in theism. Possibly we know God when we see Him, and it's not unreasonable to say that.

Another possible analogy that comes to mind to give credence to what I'm saying is the one of *love*. Sure, there's science behind some parts of love, but that's not what love is about. Science can't begin to define love for us, nor can the lab detect it. Certainly there are evidences of love, but they aren't necessarily scientific. And when somebody's in love, the only way to *prove* it is that the person who is in love says, "I know what I'm experiencing, and *I'm in love!*" There are no mathematical formulas or algorithms for it, but we accept that someone knows love when he or she experiences it. We also accept that from each other when we speak of pain (science can't measure pain), love, worry, and myriad other realities. Such is also the appropriate and acceptable measure of God.

---

[12] Ibid., p. 88

IN SUMMARY:

The following are *some* of the reasons that I feel provide good evidence for the existence of God:

- There had to have been a beginning for what we now have, and that beginning was logically outside of the reality of what now exists.
- There is an explanation for the universe that is not from its own nature.
- God's existence isn't contradictory, and so God is logically necessary.
- We have a universe and life forms that appear designed.
- It makes sense that a universe that exhibits purpose, regularity, order, and predictability did not emerge from random, unintelligent processes.
- As far as we know, information can only come from previous information, giving evidence that there is an intelligent source.
- The universe has characteristics that exhibit that its source was powerful, timeless, eternal, and intelligent.
- As far as we know, reason can only come from reason.
- As far as we know, purpose can only come from purpose.
- As far as we know, moral law is inherent in us all, and it makes sense that it came from a moral source.
- It makes sense that personality came from a personal source.
- If "shuffle" is the only mechanism in the system, "truth" can always be suspect. It makes more sense to believe that truth has truth as a source.

For Further Reading:

C.S. Lewis, Mere Christianity
Alvin Plantinga, God and Other Minds
Alvin Plantinga, Where the Conflict Really Lies

CHAPTER TWO
THE RELIABILITY OF
SCRIPTURE

The accusation is often made to me that if God really wanted to communicate with us, He would not have done it by the written word the way He did, as this person accuses: "An all-knowing, all loving, all powerful god would have the ability to communicate with his creations if he wanted to. What kind of lame deity would use written communication in an uneducated part of the world, in ancient times, when he could have just used any technology that we have available? If God's so clever why doesn't he just make a YouTube channel/ Facebook™ page/Twitter™/Pinterest™ and tell us about himself? Has he not gotten around to 'creating' Google glasses for everyone yet so we can see exactly where he is? We are more advanced now than your god ever dreamed of becoming, for the simple reason that the people who created him couldn't imagine the ways we have to communicate now."[13]

In reply, we know that any written piece of work, whether Shakespeare or the U.S. Constitution, is subject to interpretation. According to communication theory, even verbal communication and body language are subject to interpretation. There's no way around the "interpretive" part. If it's communication, there's a personal element and an interpretive element. It's the nature of the beast. Even if God

---

[13] Bobiejean, on reddit.com

spoke, dropped golden tablets into your hand, created a Facebook™ page and appeared to you in a vision, you would still have to interpret it. Since we're human, there is no other process if it's going to be both personal and universal.

But is the Bible reliable? *Reliability*, by the standards of historians, usually pertains to something that actually happened that has been discovered through verification procedures so that scholars can come to a consensus about its truth.[14] By *reliability* I mean that the Bible is historically dependable, geographically sound, culturally accurate, and theologically precise. I mean that we can count on the Bible to be giving us true-to-life information. As the God-breathed Word, I should be able to expect nothing less.

Yet the Bible is under great attack by the atheist community:

"When I read the Bible, I don't see much credibility there. At all. There are websites devoted to all the problems with the Bible. And the logic of the teaching eludes me. Parables really are the best way to confuse everyone. (40,000+ denominations). And as far as the historical evidence behind it all, I just don't see much evidence for any of it."

"The story of Christ is not even remotely original. It is instead a collection of bits and pieces from dozens of other stories that came long before. ... The Bible is full of contradictions so massive that they defy belief."

"The fact that among the most pious of men there still exists debate as to the meaning of the Bible proves that God wasn't involved in the writing of it."

"Many modern scholars claim that Matthew, Mark, Luke, and John were not the authors of the Gospels. They are all anonymous works, and were probably written long after the life of Jesus. To me it detracts from the reliability of the texts we have. They just can't be believed."

"I see no warrant to hold that the poetry and writings from many generations of an ancient civilization were anything more than stories and metaphor."

---

[14] Michael R. Licona, The Resurrection of Jesus: A New Historiographical Approach, (Downers Grove: IL, InterVarsity Press, 2010), p. 93

"How can we trust the Bible if none of the manuscripts are actually original writings, and everything we have to go off of is simply a copy of a copy of a copy? Not to mention they have been changed and altered."

These are the questions being asked. Is the Bible trustworthy? Can I reasonably claim, as I did, that the Bible is historically dependable, geographically sound, culturally accurate, and theologically precise?

It's true that the authors of very few of the books of the Bible have been proved. While traditional beliefs have much to say in their behalf, recent scholarship has called much of traditional belief into question, and without the autographs (of which we have none) and without extra-biblical corroboration (of which we have little), the authorship of the books of the Bible and their content has been subject to great debate. While a book such as this one is hardly the place to deal with the intricate details of every book of the Bible, I wish at least to give a brief summary regarding each of them.

THE QUESTION OF AUTHORSHIP

The authorship question matters. Though many may accuse that anonymity kills credibility, our lack of certainly about the author doesn't reduce its credibility any more than not knowing the author of the Hammurabi Code discredits it. But if we can attribute authority to the text because the author was a prophet spoken to by God, then the work has validity as having been God-breathed, and thus carrying spiritual authority.

There is no record that the canon of the Old Testament has ever been in doubt. Every collection has the same books, with none missing and none added. Regardless that we may not know some of the authors or the situation of their writing, the books included have without exception been recognized as authoritative.

The Pentateuch, the first five books of the Bible. In the 18th and 19th centuries, the documentary hypothesis (also called the Wellhausen hypothesis) of biblical composition arose, claiming that the Pentateuch was pieced together from four main sources (J, or Y[J]ahwist, E the

Elohist, D the Deuteronomist, and P the priestly writers). While the documentary theory gained quite a large following through the 20th century, new discoveries and research are weakening support, calling the whole theory into question, and proposing what are perceived as far more plausible alternatives.[15]

So saying, there is no end to theories about the authorship of Genesis to Deuteronomy. Many writers in the Bible, far closer in time to the days of Moses than we are, claimed that Moses is the writer (Josh. 8.31; 23.6; 1 Ki. 2.3; 2 Ki. 14.6; Mt. 8.4; 19.7; Mk .7.10, and many others). Jesus affirmed repeatedly that Moses was the author. For Christians it's generally not a matter of dispute: The biblical claims solidify Mosaic authorship.

Dr. John Walton[16] claims that though the authorship of the Pentateuch by Moses cannot be verified by evidences outside the Bible, it is clear that he was considered the authority behind the five books we have. His words, teachings, and actions can be considered to be represented with accuracy in the biblical text. As the leader of the people, "Moses was generating information...that would be considered important enough to preserve in written documents. Some undoubtedly would have been recorded in his time[17] and under his supervision. Others may well have been produced by later generations after some time of oral transmission. It matters neither how much material is in each category nor which portions are which; the authority derives from Moses and he is inseparable from the material."[18] Even if Moses didn't actually *write* it,[19] there is no verified reason to doubt that the material is his, even if it was not actually put to paper (parchment) until much later.

---

[15] R.N. Whybray, Hans Heinrich Schmid, Rolf Rendtorff, Erhard Blum, John Van Seters, et al. Oswald T. Allis's *The Five Books of Moses* (1943) effectively demolished the Documentary Hypothesis.

[16] John H. Walton & D. Brent Sandy, The Lost World of Scripture, (Downers Grove, IL: IVP Academic, 2013), pp. 60-61

[17] Several passages from the first five books (Ex. 15; Numbers 23-24; Gn. 49; Dt. 32-33, for instance) have been verified as being extremely old, coming from the era when Moses is believed to have lived

[18] Walton & Sandy, Op. Cit., pp. 60-61

[19] Since Moses was raised as Egyptian royalty, it's unknown whether or not he would have been taught how to write.

Joshua. The book is anonymous. It makes no claims either for authorship or for the date it was written. Some of the themes and stylistic elements point to the late 7th century (around 620 BC) or later, while there are content elements that would suggest a date before 1000.[20] Since the book makes no claims about its writer or date of writing, the question of authorship is moot as to its reliability, so the book needs to be weighed based on the accuracy of its contents, which are verifiably accurate, not on the identification of the author.

Judges. The book is anonymous and it makes no claims either for authorship or for the date it was written. References in the book place its writing between about 1100-1000 BC. The evidences that allow accurate dating of the book are so scant and sparse that this book is not used in the reliability of Scripture debate, either pro or con. While there are opinions about historical accuracy, this era in Canaan, Israel, Egypt and Mesopotamia is one of the least known eras of the ancient world (Iron Age I). Until more information comes to light, *Judges* is not a major factor in evaluating the reliability of Scripture.

The Historical Books: Samuel, Kings, Chronicles. Again, the authorship and dates of writing of the historical books are not the objects of reliability debates about the Bible. More pertinent to those discussions in these books is the confirmable historicity of the accounts and their concurrence with what archaeologists are digging up. Who the authors are is unknown and most likely unknowable, but that doesn't change any conversations about the reliability of the documents.

Ezra-Nehemiah. No one knows who wrote the books of Ezra and Nehemiah. Many scholars say they were written sometime during the 5th century BC. Whether or not that is true, it's still quite possible that the information in them came from Ezra and Nehemiah themselves.

Esther. The book makes no claims of authorship or for the date it was written. There is little evidence to substantiate any theories. It

---

[20] Joshua 8.32; 13.6; 15.63; 16.10

was obviously written after the 5th century BC, and the setting of the narrative and analysis of the language indicates it's older than the 2nd century BC,[21] but other than that nothing is known. The discussion of Esther's reliability is more about the content than its source. There is no extrabiblical corroboration of any elements of the narrative. That, of course, doesn't guarantee that the story is false, only that it is unverified.

Job. Job is possibly the oldest book of the Bible, since the elements in its poetry relate most accurately to the patriarchal period (the time of Abraham, Isaac, and Jacob), roughly from about 2000–1700 BC. There is little historical information in the book to help determine a date. There is strong evidence that it was written by a single author, but there are debates about some sections of Job coming from other authors. Since the book is poetry and the theme is theological/philosophical, the date and author of the book are immaterial, and questions about it being historically reliable are moot. "The lack of information [about its author and date of writing] does not affect our interpretation of the book."[22]

Psalms. The book of Psalms is a mixed bag, because no one contends that they were all authored by the same person, or even during the same era. Some psalms claim to be written by David in about 1000 BC, some by Moses (ca. 1500-1300 BC?), while others are anonymous and are clearly written after 540 BC (e.g. Pss. 126, 137). Archaeology is able to "confirm an early date for the first book and a late date for the fifth book."[23] It is widely accepted that the Psalms were not assembled in their present form before 500 BC. Seventy-three of the psalms are attributed (by title) to David. Other authors are said to have been Moses, Solomon, Asaph, Heman, Ethan, and the group called the sons of Korah.[24] It is impossible to know the accuracy of the

---

[21] Andrew Hill and John Walton, A Survey of the Old Testament, (Zondervan Publishing House, Grand Rapids, MI, 1991, 2000, 2009), p. 349

[22] John Walton, The NIV Application Commentary: Job (Zondervan Publishing House, Grand Rapids, MI, 2012) p. 23

[23] Mitchell First, "Can Archaeology Help Date the Psalms?", *Biblical Archaeology Review*, July/August 2012, p. 54

[24] Hill & Walton, Op. Cit. p. 421

titles (and therefore the authors), and whether those labels (or some of them) are meant to designate the author or the person to whom the psalm is dedicated.

Proverbs. Proverbs as a genre are generally sayings passed as humor and advice through a culture by word of mouth. They are often not written down in an anthology until someone (an editor) decides to collect and preserve them. Most of the Proverbs are attributed to Solomon (Prov. 1.1), whom the Bible credits with widely recognized wisdom (1 Ki. 4.29-34). "It seems reasonable and defensible to recognize Solomon's hand in the book, but it is also important to honor the other clear compositional indications."[25] Many of the proverbs (namely chapters 10-22.16 and chapters 22-29) date to the era of Solomon (989-932 BC), while others are explicitly attributed to other authors (30.1; 31.1; 22.17-24.23). The proverbs in chapters 1-9 could have a source in Solomon, though perhaps they were not written down until the era of Hezekiah.[26] The collection was most likely assembled in the 6th century BC.

"The notion of 'dating' a text…is not quite germane to the book of Proverbs. The book by its own testimony is a collection of sayings from an indefinite number of [authors] (see 24.23) over a number of generations, at a minimum from Solomon's time (mid-tenth century) to Hezekiah's (eighth to seventh centuries; see 25.1)."[27]

Ecclesiastes. The author claims to be a "son of David" and "king in Jerusalem". It may very well be that Solomon is the author, but it's not necessary. What is more likely is that the writer put his book "into Solomon's mouth as a didactic device. … The sermon is certainly Solomonic in the sense that it teaches lessons that Solomon had unique opportunities to learn."[28] "Son of David" also doesn't necessarily mean a direct son, but could be any one of David's descendants. Solomon

---

[25] Tremper Longman III, *Proverbs*, Baker Commentary on the Old Testament Wisdom and Psalms (Tremper Longman III, editor), (Grand Rapids, MI, Baker Academic, 2006) p. 24

[26] Hill & Walton, Op. Cit. p. 443

[27] Michael V. Fox, Proverbs 1-9, The Anchor Bible Vol. 18A (Doubleday: New York, 2000) p. 6

[28] J.I. packer, Knowing God (Downers Grove, IL: InterVarsity Press, 1973), p. 93

thus possibly becomes the symbolic author of the work,[29] though it's completely possible that he is the true and direct author of it. While it is not impossible that Solomon was the writer, it doesn't make sense that as king he would write anonymously. The date of the book's writing is therefore unknown, and there is nothing in the book's contents to give a clue about when it was written.

Song of Solomon. Though Solomon's name is used seven times in the book, there's no guarantee that he wrote it. He may indeed have been the author, or the original source of the material—the authority figure connected with the work, or the subject of its dedication. It's also possible that he is merely written into the book as its key figure (Solomon only appears in the book in the third person). There are elements of the story and terminology that fit Solomon's time, but other scholars place the writing much later. Given all the uncertainties, we have to consider the author and the era of the work as presently undeterminable.

Isaiah. The authorship of Isaiah is academically complex and highly debated. It is probably best to understand Isaiah similarly to the Pentateuch: Isaiah can easily be seen as the authority figure behind the writings and prophecies of the book. There is no reason to suspect he didn't write much of it down himself, though other sections may have been transcribed by persons with him, and possibly others were added in later years as the prophecies of Isaiah were all compiled into one volume. It's also very possible that Isaiah wrote it all. The New Testament repeatedly affirms Isaiah as the author of his prophecy, which would give not only evidence but inspiration to regard Isaiah as the author. None of the disagreements detracts from Isaiah being both the direct source and the authority of the writings that have been put in his name.

Jeremiah. Regardless of the fact that Jeremiah provides direct information about its author and date, academic speculations about both span a vast breadth of eras with little agreement. Internal evidence would put the writing in about 604 BC (Jer. 36.18, 32). The

[29] Jacques Ellul, *Reason for Being: A Meditation on Ecclesiastes* (Grand Rapids, MI, Wm. B. Eerdmans Publishing Company, 1990) p. 20

end of Jeremiah speaks of the invasion by Babylon in 586. Debates about literary forms, writing styles, and terminology cause endless theorizing about a variety of writers over centuries of time. Until further information becomes available, we can at least consider, as previously, that Jeremiah is the authority behind the writing of his book, and there is good reason to affirm Jeremiah himself as the author of the book.

Lamentations. No one knows who wrote Lamentations, nor when it was written. The book is poetic and makes no claim of authorship or date. Since it laments the fall of Jerusalem to the Babylonians in 586 BC, it is often thought to have been written then, which is entirely believable. Tradition holds that Jeremiah is the author, and that is also quite possible.

Ezekiel. The authorship of Ezekiel is much debated, but there are good reasons to believe that it was indeed penned by Ezekiel himself. The book is filled with references to Ezekiel in the first person, and he claims to have been writing what the Lord told him. The context and language are appropriate to the era and location of Ezekiel. He dates a number of the prophecies to the year, month, and day, making it more probable he is the true author.

Daniel. The book is anonymous, though the prophecies inside it are claimed to be the visions and prophecies of Daniel. It is often argued that the book could not have been written before 168 BC, because that would mean that it actually prophesied about the future. There is, however, no direct evidence that the book was not or could not have been written in the late 500s BC during the life of Daniel, and by Daniel.

Hosea. The book claims to be the work of the prophet Hosea, and there is every good reason to believe it. The historical context, language, and themes all fit the 720s-730s BC when Hosea lived, and no credible evidence has been assembled to disprove that assumption.

Joel. The book is undated and claims to be the work of the prophet Joel. All discussions about dating and authorship come from internal analyses and the subsequent educated opinions. A tug of war debates whether it was written in about 800 BC in the time of Joel, during the postexilic period (around 500 BC), or somewhere between them. The debate rages on and will not be settled until more evidence comes to light. As with Isaiah, that the book was written down in later years doesn't mean that Joel is not the prophetic voice of authority behind the prophecies written in his name.

Amos. The book claims to be the work of Amos, and it contains several first-person accounts. The writing style and history are consistent with the time of Amos, and no substantial evidence has been mounted to doubt that Amos was truly the author or at least the one who dictated the material. "Many scholars agree that the prophecy of Amos is, at least in essence, an authentic production of the man whose name it bears."[30]

Obadiah. "Obadiah contains no information about the time or place of its origin, nor does it include any autobiographical data about the prophet and author."[31] Scholars have dated it anywhere over a 400-year span, from about 850-400 BC. There's no direct evidence to doubt that Obadiah was the author.

Jonah. No author is identified in the book. It is the story of Jonah and his prophetic call, but it doesn't claim to have been written by Jonah. While it may have been written by Jonah, another possibility is that Jonah passed his story on to others, who may have passed it to others, and eventually it was written down. This makes Jonah the authority behind the writing of the book, but its author is unknown.

Micah. The language, themes, and context of the book fit the era in which Micah lived and prophesied, and no convincing information

---

[30] Tremper Longman III & David E. Garland, *The Expositor's Bible Commentary (Revised Edition): Daniel – Malachi* (Grand Rapids, MI: Zondervan Publishing Co., 2008), p. 350

[31] Hill & Walton, Op. Cit. p. 620

has been brought out that would create a reasonable doubt that Micah indeed wrote the book.

Nahum. There is very little in the book to allow much evidence of who the author is and when it was written. There is no reason to doubt Nahum's authorship, but there's no particular evidence besides Nahum 1.1 to establish his authorship.

Habakkuk. The book has enough consistent language and style to be attributed to one author. No substantial evidence has been mounted to doubt that Habakkuk is that author.

Zephaniah. "We do not actually know for sure whether Zephaniah personally composed this book. Perhaps he did, but perhaps he entrusted the task to a faithful scribe, in a manner similar to Jeremiah's use of Baruch (Jer. 36.4; cf. Rom. 16.22). 'The word of the Lord that came to Zephaniah' (Zeph. 1.1) indicates that the contents are substantially what Zephaniah received. But is the order and arrangement of the materials directly from Zephaniah, or partly to a later scribe or disciple(s)? Did he communicate his work orally, or write it down at the time? Ultimately, we don't have definite information about the final composition of the book."[32]

Haggai. The book itself is silent on the issue of authorship, and most of the book is written in the third person.[33] While it is entirely possible that Haggai penned the prophecy, it is not necessarily so, though it is universally accepted that the writing comes from the time of the life of Haggai. No book of the Bible is more explicitly dated than Haggai.

Zechariah. There is little debate that the first eight chapters were written by Zechariah. Opinion is sharply divided over the rest of the book, however.

---

[32] Vern Poythress, "Dispensing with Human Meaning..." JETS 57/3 (Sept 2014), pp. 482-484

[33] Hill & Walton, Op. cit., p. 678

Malachi. There is no explicit claim to authorship, only that the book expresses the prophecies of Malachi. The language and style of the book fit well with the 6th century BC when Malachi was thought to have lived. Scholars feel for certain that it was composed some time after 538 BC.[34] There is no basis for a claim that it was authored by anyone other than Malachi.

THE NEW TESTAMENT

The four Gospels are the most fought over territory of the Bible, so I have given them more attention. There is a great effort on the part of some people to discredit the authorship (source) and dating of the Gospel accounts, to steal away their authority and reliability. The Gospels, however, can be supported as both authentic and reliable.

Matthew. Matthew, like all of the Gospels, is anonymous. It was the nature of the genre, as it is with modern novels, not to put one's name in the body of the work. Its anonymity has no effect on its authenticity, though it has created much debate. As with many such authorial issues, we have to infer the most logical conclusion rather than insist on ultimate proof.

The superscription "According to Matthew" is on every edition that has been found, from the earliest (starting around AD 200) and through the centuries. There is no copy of Matthew without his name on it. Papias of Hierapolis, writing in about AD 125-130, attributed it to Matthew, as did Irenaeus, also in the second century. The early church fathers were unanimous in attributing it to Matthew. There has been no debate over authorship until modern times.

Modern scholarship doubts Matthew's authorship on the basis that the author seemed to have used source material (perhaps Mark or the mysteriously speculated "Q" document, still unproved); the claim is that one of Jesus' disciples would not have needed source material, having been an eyewitness. Besides that, they argue, Mark wasn't even an eyewitness! The truth remains, however, that even as an eyewitness, he could have written the stories the way they were

[34] Longman & Garland, Op. Cit., p 837

circulating at the time and not have felt that to be compromising his integrity as an author or as an eyewitness. There is substantial evidence that Matthew could easily have been the author.[35]

- The author seems to have been a highly educated Jew, as was Matthew, a tax collector.
- The author was familiar with technical aspects of the Jewish law, as was Matthew, or Levi, probably of the priestly tribe.
- The interest of the Gospel in the Law, in ecclesiastical matters, and in oral interpretation of law and custom, would come most readily from a man trained in the legal disciplines, or from one who had been in constant touch with men trained in them. Matthew the Jew, who was also a tax collector and most likely a Levite, fits that profile.
- The Gospel's parables reflect interest in the spiritual history of Israel as God's chosen people, a concern that would be expected of a Levite.
- The level of Greek fits a man who was a native Palestinian but who regularly did business in the Greek language.
- Mark is not necessarily a source for Matthew. Recent scholarship has called into question both the traditional view that Matthew got his material from Mark, as well as the existence of the "Q" document, of which no part or evidence has ever been found. A few scholars now are proposing that Matthew was written before Mark, and Mark was possibly an abbreviated rendition of Matthew. Despite the similarities between the two Gospels, there are so many differences between the two accounts in the way they are written and what they include, it's obvious that they didn't just copy from each other.[36]

While not much information is available, all of the known elements serve to convince us that we are dealing with an author

---

[35] Some of the material on this list came from Albright & Mann, *the Anchor Bible: Matthew* Vol. 26, pp. CLXXXIII-CLXXXIV

[36] Richard B. Hays, *The Moral Vision of the New Testament* (New York, NY: Harper One, 1996) pp. 93-94

very similar to what we would expect Matthew to be like.[37] There is no evidence from the early centuries that it was ever doubted that Matthew was its writer, and every piece of evidence available points to him.

Mark. Mark is also anonymous, but the evidence for Mark's authorship is also substantial.

We know from the book of Acts that Mark traveled with Paul and Barnabas, who was his cousin (Col. 4.10), on a missionary journey (Acts 12.25), and then embarked on another trip with Barnabas in Acts 15.39. Sometime later he rejoined Paul and traveled with him (Col. 4.10; 2 Tim. 4.11; Philemon 1.24). It is therefore quite reasonable to assume that Mark had possibly met some of the apostles, since Paul met them on occasion. Mark also seems to have been a traveling companion of the apostle Peter (1 Pet. 5.13, where Peter calls him "my son"). Therefore we know that Mark had secondhand information about the life and ministry of Jesus.

It's also likely that Mark had firsthand information about Jesus. He is first mentioned by name in Acts 12.12 (and again in 12.25) as a resident of Jerusalem where his mother, Mary, seems to have been an important part of the Christian community. These facts indicate that Mark was most likely a teenager or a young man during the ministry of Jesus, possibly living in or near Jerusalem, and since his mother was a believer, it's an easy step to think that Mark possibly had some firsthand exposure to the person of Jesus. Even modern scholarship considers the stories contained in Mark to have come from the inner circle of the disciples.[38]

As to the Gospel that bears his name, the superscription "According to Mark" exists on most extant manuscripts, and the early church fathers were unanimous in attributing the writing of it to Mark. There is substantial evidence that Mark could have been the author.

- The early church fathers unanimously recognized Mark as the author.

---

[37] Albright & Mann, *the Anchor Bible: Matthew* Vol. 26, pp. CLXXXIII-CLXXXIV
[38] Ezra P. Gould, International Critical Commentary Series on the Holy Scriptures of the Old and New Testaments: The Gospel According to St. Mark (Edinburgh, Scotland: T. & T. Clark, 1982), p. xliii

- It doesn't make sense that anyone would have pasted the name of Mark on a Gospel if he were not the author. What makes more sense is that they would have attributed it to Peter or James if they were trying to ascribe credibility to the work. There is no reason anyone would have attached Mark's name to the book unless he had actually written it.
- The use of Aramaic words and phrases in the book are evidence that the author lived in Palestine.
- The use of biblical quotations and allusions to prophecy imply that the author was Jewish and had been trained in the knowledge of the Scriptures.
- The gospel has similarities to items and emphases that also occur in Paul's writings, attesting that the author may have been acquainted with the apostle Paul.
- The quality of the Greek in the book is only average, consistent with what can be expected from Palestinian Jews of the era, for whom Greek was a second (or third) language.
- The Gentile orientation of the Gospel could be evidence that it was written by someone who had traveled in the Gentile world. (Peter is believed to have been in Rome from AD 55-60 [an argument by W.T. Manson], and Mark may have been there with him.) The Gospel has Latin words transliterated into Greek (Mk. 15.39), and Jewish customs are explained as if a Gentile audience may be unfamiliar with them (Mk. 7.3-5).

There is no evidence from the first century that it was ever doubted that Mark was the writer of Mark, and the argument is strong for his authorship.

Luke. Luke is anonymous, as are all of the Gospels. Luke was a friend and traveling companion of Paul's, so would have had access through Paul to any of his experiences or the information he had picked up from the apostles and others. Luke claims in the introduction of his Gospel to have interviewed many people with the goal of presenting a reliable historical account of what actually happened.

What evidence do we have that Luke was the author?

1. The uniform testimony of the early church is that Luke was the author.[39]
2. There are numerous technical medical terms in the gospel,[40] consistent with Dr. Luke (Col. 4.14) as the author.[41]
3. The Greek in Luke has a high quality consistent with a Gentile author.
4. His limited knowledge of Palestinian geography and customs betrays that he is not a Palestinian.
5. He claims not to have been an eyewitness, but to have gotten his information from others, which is consistent with Luke.
6. The author was well educated.
7. The author was acquainted with both Old Testament literary traditions and Hellenistic literary techniques.[42]
8. The title "According to Luke" is on the oldest extant manuscripts.

There is little to no evidence offered from scholarship that Luke was not the author.

John. The Gospel of John is anonymous along with the other Gospels. Examining the evidence for its date of writing yields the first challenge. There are almost no clues in the book itself to help, so all guesses at its date of writing are interpretive educated guesses. Scholarly evidences can provide a case for a wide range of possibilities.

The early church fathers regarded it as the latest of the four. A papyrus fragment of it from sometime between AD 100-150 is in existence, so that's the latest it could have been written, but a late date has not been proved. Most scholars put its writing in the 90s, but that can't be firmly established. Here are some of the evidences for an early writing:

---

[39] Ravi Zacharias & Norman Geisler (ed.), Who Made God? (Grand Rapids, MI: Zondervan, 2003), p. 75-81
[40] "Taken" with a "great fever" (Lk. 4.38); "full of sores"; "in great pain" (16.20-25); "great drops of blood" (22.44).
[41] G. Coleman Luck, *Luke: The Gospel of the Son of Man* (Chicago, IL: Moody Press, 1960), p. 13
[42] Fitzmyer, The Anchor Bible Vol. 28, *Luke I-IX*, p. 35

- There is no mention of the destruction of the temple in AD 70.
- The author doesn't seem to be aware of the existence of the other three Gospels.
- Some of the expressions in the Gospel seem early, such as calling the followers of Jesus "disciples" (instead of "apostles"), and the way he refers to "the Jews."
- The author's concern over the followers of John the Baptist is a very early concern.

So who wrote this Gospel?

Reasons against John as the author:

- The style of the book is very different from the style of Matthew and Mark, even though John would have been a contemporary of theirs and friends with both of them.
- Some scholars consider that the Gospel is filled with Gnostic[43] language, proving that John was not the author (though the style of writing has not been proved to be Gnostic).
- Describing oneself as "the disciple whom Jesus loved" is deemed unnatural.
- Most of the stories of the Gospel take place in Judea. John was from Galilee.
- There is no mention of the Transfiguration or of Jesus' agony in the Garden of Gethsemane, for both of which John was present.
- No name is attributed to the gospel in its earliest days.

Reasons to accept John as the author:

- Theophilus of Antioch (c. AD 180) identifies John as the author.
- Irenaeus (who says he got his information from Polycarp, who knew John personally) identifies John as the author.
- Clement of Alexandria (AD 150-215) identifies John as the author.
- Tertullian (AD 155-240) considered John to be the author.
- The statement of John 21.24 ("This is the disciple who testifies

---

[43] Gnosticism was an ancient religious system emphasizing, among other tenets, the spiritual over the material.

to these things and who wrote them down. We know that his testimony is true.") affirms John's authorship.

- The description and character of "the disciple whom Jesus loved" fits what we know about John, the disciple of Jesus:
  - ▷ A close friendship with Jesus
  - ▷ Jesus' mother was put in his care (19.26-27, 34-35)
  - ▷ Racing with Peter to the tomb (20.2-5)
  - ▷ Recognizing Jesus on the shore (21.7)
  - ▷ Present at the Last Supper, where only the 12 were present (Mt. 26.20)
  - ▷ A close friendship with Peter (13.24; 20.2; 21.7)
- John was a son of Zebedee (21.2)
- If the Gospel had been written by someone else, he most likely would have mentioned John's name to bolster the credibility of the book.
- The writer knew Palestine and its culture well.
  - ▷ The connection of Elijah with Jewish messianic expectations (1.21)
  - ▷ The low view held of women (4.27)
  - ▷ The importance attaching to the religious schools (7.15)
  - ▷ The hostility between Jews and Samaritans (4.9)
  - ▷ The contempt the Pharisees had for ordinary people (7.49)
  - ▷ The importance of the Sabbath and its rules (5.10)
  - ▷ The need to circumcise a child overrode the Sabbath (7.22-23)
- He knew the topography of Palestine
  - ▷ Cana of Galilee is mentioned in no earlier writing known to us
- The writing style is that of a Jew of Palestinian culture
- Many texts have the touch of an eyewitness
  - ▷ Times of day that have no bearing on the plot or narrative (1.39; 4.6, etc.)
  - ▷ A link of Jesus' behavior with one of the feasts (2.13, 23, etc.)
  - ▷ Place names are brought in naturally and for no apparent reason other than narrative events

> ▷ The call of the disciples (1.35-51)
> ▷ The episode of the foot-washing (13.1-20)
> ▷ Information about persons not mentioned elsewhere: Nicodemus, Malchus, Annas
> ▷ Claims to eyewitness testimony (1.14; 19.35)

- The controversies are 1st century controversies, not the kinds of question discussed in the 2nd century[44]
  > ▷ The use and abuse of Sabbath (ch. 5)
  > ▷ The Messiah and his credentials (6.15; 11.47-50)
  > ▷ True and false Judaism
- The writer had an inner knowledge of the apostles
  > ▷ Conversations (4.33; 16.17; 20.25; 21.3, 7)
  > ▷ Thoughts (2.11, 17, 22; 4.27; 6.19, 60-61)
  > ▷ Places they frequented (11.54; 18.2)
  > ▷ Mistakes they made that were later corrected (2.21-22; 11.13; 12.16)
- The Gospel was universally accepted as canonical because people were convinced it was written by John.

The case for John's authorship is far stronger than the case against it. There is also no evidence from the 1st century that John as the author of John was ever in doubt.

The stronger evidence is that all four Gospels could have been written within forty years of Jesus' life and death, that they were written while eyewitnesses were still alive, and that there are many evidences of eyewitness accounts within the narrative. It's no different than today writing about the Nixon presidency, the Vietnam War, or the Beatles. Plenty of people are still alive who can vouch for the accuracy of many of the facts. It's not so far away in history that we can reasonably conclude that all mention of it is fictional.

Acts. Reasonable arguments favor the identification of Luke as the author of Acts.

- The internal evidence supports Luke as the author
  > ▷ Some passages are written in the first person plural,

---

[44] 2nd century discussions were about the episcopacy, Gnostic emanations, the date of keeping Easter, etc.

plausibly from the mind and pen of Luke, a companion of Paul.

> ▷ The second part of the book has evidences of direct, firsthand knowledge of the events being described, consistent with a fellow-worker and traveling companion of Paul.

• Every attestation of the early church and the church fathers is that Luke is the author. There is no evidence of any other author: Luke's authorship is uncontested.

• Acts was most likely written by a Gentile Christian.

• The author emphasized details and used terminology characteristic of a physician.

No sustainable argument has been offered that seriously puts Luke's authorship of Acts in question or in doubt.

Romans. The writer of Romans identifies himself as Paul (1.1). Being quoted by the church fathers guarantees an early date of writing. It is unanimously attested to Paul by the early church, and almost unanimously attributed to Paul by modern scholars. Paul's authorship of Romans is one of the most solid and unquestioned authorship facts of the entire Bible.

1 Corinthians. Like Romans, modern scholars have joined historians in almost unanimously concluding that Paul is the author of 1 Corinthians. The letter is quoted or mentioned by the earliest of sources and is included in every ancient canon. The date of writing is thought to be AD 54-57, and the author is confidently Paul of Tarsus.

2 Corinthians. This is another book that scholars put solidly in the camp of Paul's authorship. It has the same style, vocabulary, and content as the other confirmed writings of Paul, and its authorship is as certain as that of any historic work can be. "The evidence, both external and internal, for the Pauline authorship of this letter is so strong as to be irrefragable" (indisputable).[45] It was probably written in AD 56-57.

---

[45] Philip E. Hughes, Commentary on the Second Epistle to the Corinthians, The International Commentary on the New Testament, (Grand Rapids, MI: Wm. B. Eerdmans Publishing Co., 1962) p. xv

Galatians. The internal evidence for Paul as the author is strong, with his name occurring throughout the letter and the inclusion of an abundance of autobiographical information. With much personal and specific information, it's not a letter that might have been written by anyone else and ascribed to Paul. External evidence also points to Paul as the author, with all of the church fathers ascribing authorship to Paul. It was accepted as Pauline by the early church. "Galatians, therefore, with few exceptions, is accepted as Pauline by the conservative and radical critics alike."[46]

Ephesians. Many of the early church fathers (Clement of Rome, Ignatius, Hermas, and Polycarp) support Paul's authorship. "By the close of the second century the Epistle was universally received as St. Paul's."[47] Though some modern scholars (of the past two centuries) have questioned Pauline authorship, the authenticity of it is amply sustained by evidence, both external and internal.[48] Despite the critics' persistent doubts about Paul's authorship of Ephesians, their arguments are inconclusive and stand against all of the early attestation. "If the maxim 'innocent until proven guilty'…is applied here, then the tradition that accepts Paul as the author of Ephesians is more recommendable than the suggestion of an unknown author. The burden of proof lies with those questioning the tradition. The evidence produced by them is neither strong nor harmonious enough to invalidate the judgment of tradition. Although it cannot be definitively proved that Ephesians is genuinely Pauline, nevertheless it is still possible to uphold its authenticity."[49]

Philippians. "The Letter [to the Philippians] asserts the authorship of Paul (1.1), and there is nothing in the Letter, linguistic or historical, which can cause any doubt as to its authenticity."[50] The

---

[46] Merrill Tenney, *Galatians: The Charter of Christian Liberty* (Grand Rapids, MI: Wm. B. Eerdmans Publishing Co., 1950) p. 45

[47] T.K. Abbott, *A Critical and Exegetical Commentary: Epistles to the Ephesians and to the Colossians* (T.& T. Clark: Edinburgh, United Kingdom, 1991) p. xii

[48] E.K. Simpson, Ephesians: The New Testament International Commentary on the New Testament, (Grand Rapids, MI: Wm. B. Eerdmans Publishing Co., 1957), p. 17

[49] Marcus Barth and Helmut Blanke, *Colossians*, The Anchor Bible Volume 34b (New York, NY: Doubleday, 1994) p. 125

[50] Jac J. Muller, *The Epistles of Paul to the Philippians and to Philemon* (Grand Rapids, MI: Wm. B. Erdmans Publishing Co., 1955) p. 14

evidence for Paul's authorship is both early and strong. The only serious doubt about Paul's authorship of Philippians was mounted in the mid-19th century, and it has been found to have been in error. Very few scholars today doubt Pauline authorship of it.

Colossians. There is no substantial external evidence that Paul is not the writer, and his authorship was not challenged from that aspect until the 1800s. It is argued that the vocabulary and style are not distinctively Pauline, but it must also be remembered that Paul was writing to a church he had not visited, and which had issues that no other church had previously had, so one might expect some uniqueness. In addition, the similarities of vocabulary and subject matter with Ephesians are strong arguments for Pauline authorship. "In consequence, the most solid and safest working hypothesis for the reading and exposition of Colossians is still the assumption that it was Paul who wrote, or rather dictated, the whole letter himself, and that eventual revisions, made by one or several aides before its delivery to those addressed, were executed at his command or with his approval."[51]

1 & 2 Thessalonians. There is very little dispute about Paul being the author of 1 & 2 Thessalonians. By common scholarly consent, they date to about AD 49/50.

1 & 2 Timothy, Titus. Many modern scholars doubt that Paul actually wrote the Pastoral Epistles to Timothy and Titus, though other scholars actively disagree and attribute the books to him. The books use many of Paul's terms, phrases, and style, however, and could easily have been written by him to good friends towards the end of his life. The debate will rage for many years to come, but the evidence is in Paul's favor.

Philemon. There is almost no dispute about Paul being the writer of Philemon.

---

[51] Marcus Barth and Helmut Blanke, *Colossians*, The Anchor Bible Volume 34b (New York, NY: Doubleday, 1994) p. 125

Hebrews. Hebrews makes no statement of any claim of authorship. Its author is unknown. Some church fathers attributed it to Clement, others to Paul, but there was no consensus as with other books. Tertullian argued that Barnabas might have been the author. There has never been any agreement about who the author was, and the book itself takes no stance. Once again, the lack of a known author doesn't make the book any less true.

James. Traditionally, the author of the book is James, the brother of Jesus, the leader of the church in Jerusalem. The very first verse admits to an author named *James*, but James was a common name in first-century Palestine. The book appears to be completely unknown in most of the second century, and doesn't appear on a canon list until AD 170. Origen (AD 184-253) attributes the writing to Jesus' brother, and Jerome includes the book in the Vulgate[52] in AD 385. Many of the early writers[53] say it was written by James, Jesus' brother. The author is no doubt a Jew with a commanding knowledge of the Old Testament and a familiarity with the Septuagint. He is versed in Hellenism and is a thoughtful and intelligent writer. Throughout history the identity of the author has been debated, and no certain determination is forthcoming. "Most scholars agree that the best candidate for 'James' in the Greeting (1.1) is James of Jerusalem, called by Paul 'the Brother of the Lord' (Gal. 1.19)."[54] Regardless, the book doesn't claim to be written by an eyewitness, or by Jesus' brother, or by an apostle, so the authority of the book is not changed by knowing or not knowing the author.

1 Peter. Modern scholars generally believe that Peter is not the author of 1 Peter. By contrast, the writers in the early church[55] unanimously attributed it to him. It is widely quoted, and it is considered to be a very early document (AD 58-64). There are substantial arguments mounted from both sides of the discussion. Another possibility is that Peter dictated the letter to Silvanus (or

---

[52] Jerome's translation of the Bible in Latin

[53] Chrysostom, Andrew of Crete, Rufinus, Prosper of Aquitaine, Gregory of Tours, Bede, Bar-Hebraeus

[54] Luke Timothy Johnson, "The Letter of James," The Anchor Bible Vol. 37A (New York, NY: Doubleday, 1995), p. 92

[55] Irenaeus, Tertullian, Clement of Alexandria, Origen of Alexandria

Silas, 1 Pet. 5.12), who put Peter's words in proper Greek. The issue may never be resolved, though the strength of evidence falls to the testimony of the early church, which considered it to be written by Peter.

2 Peter. The authorship of 2 Peter is a hot debate. Even the early church questioned the inclusion of the book in the New Testament. 2 Peter 1:1 claims the Apostle Peter, Simon Peter, as its author. Since it ended up being accepted as a canonical book, the early church recognized its authority. The questions about the authenticity of it were based on the similarity of chapter 2 to the book of Jude, not on any inconsistency of vocabulary or style (with which the early church would have been much more familiar than we are). It is said by modern scholars that the writing is too Hellenistic for Peter, that the vocabulary differs from 1 Peter too much, and that the issues dealt with in the book are not from Peter's sphere. It's also possible that Peter became more familiar with the Gentile world in his travels, and learned from his experiences. It's impossible to say conclusively at this point who wrote the book, but Peter is not a stretch.

Jude. Jude claims to be a brother of James, presumably (but not necessarily) the James who was a leader in the early church who was a brother of Jesus, making Jude a brother of Jesus also. Could this be so? If so, he, like his brother James, neglected to mention this in the introduction to his book. The authenticity of the book was never doubted by the early church. There is very little to provide evidence in one direction or the other, so the traditional interpretation should stand until convincing evidence dislodges that position.

Revelation. The author identifies himself as John, yet gives us no help to know which John, or much about this John. Some scholars speculate that it was John Mark, others John the prophet, and still others John the Elder or even John the Baptist. Early tradition[56] is unanimous in its opinion that it was written by the Apostle John.[57]

---

[56] Justin Martyr, Clement of Alexandria, Tertullian, the Apocryphon of John

[57] Robert H. Mounce, *The New International Commentary on the New Testament: The Book of Revelation* (Grand Rapids, MI: William B. Eerdmans Publishing Co., 1977) p. 27

A number of linguistic similarities exist between the Gospel of John and the book of Revelation. "Guthrie argues that there are internal considerations which pose serious difficulties if authorship is denied to the apostle John."[58] All of the evidence is debated, but there is no argument strong enough to disprove "John's" authorship. To be fair, there's little evidence to prove it as well. The book itself doesn't claim to be written by the apostle, and so if it were written by another John, it does not undermine its authority.

MY CONCLUSION

The bottom line is that, unless you are a hard-core minimalist, the reliability of the Bible is augmented by the authorship data, not discredited. The evidences against traditional perspectives on authorship are not strong enough to justify a condemning conclusion. While the Bible is continually being studied, and new analyses are always being done, for now the Bible stands quite solidly on grounds of its authority as has been traditionally held. Just because documents close to the proposed date of writing don't exist is insufficient to prove that the book is not both ancient and attributable to its traditional author.

OTHER FACTORS OF BIBLICAL RELIABILITY

The standards of reliability for the biblical text are no different than for any other historical text. The Bible doesn't get its own set of rules when it comes to validity. Many critics claim that if the text is not reliable in historical matters, it shows that God allowed his writers to say things that were wrong, and therefore it is not a divine text.

The first question to ask, therefore, is how can we determine that any historical text is reliable? Here is a suggested list of criteria:

---

[58] Ibid. p. 30

1. What is claimed corroborates with other historical records we have regarding the same material: culture, history, chronology, geography, persons, and events. The more records we have, the closer we can come to an agreement about what actually happened.
2. Early and independent attestation gives more credibility. The closer we can get to the original document, the more potential there is that we have an accurate text, and more possibly written by the author claimed.
3. What is written must make sense in the historical picture. To claim that Alexander the Great invented the airplane is too wild to believe, even if an ancient historian wrote it.
4. Evaluate the evidence that is available regarding author, date of writing, the age of the evidence, and the method and dependability of transmission.
5. We would expect similarity of culture and terminology between the writing and its era.

It must be affirmed that regardless of sensibility and corroboration, none of this, whether biblical or secular, is foolproof. The records we have are all subject to interpretation, and we have to play with the cards in our hand. Monopolizing Knowledge by Ian Hutchinson[59] says that though "historians claim scientific norms of historiography, the effort is not convincing."[60] All it means is that historiography is not science, but interpretation. All historians are interpreters of limited information, and their reliability rises and falls with both the quantity of information and the subjective quality of their interpretations.

These are the claims of reliability I am making about the Bible:

1. The writers of the Bible fully considered that they were communicating the very words of God and authentic theological interpretations of historical events. While we can debate about their success or failure, their intent was reliable historiography and theological accuracy.
2. The discovery of the Dead Sea Scrolls confirms that the transmission of the biblical text over the centuries is amazingly

---

[59] Ian Hutchinson, Monopolizing Knowledge (Belmont, MA: Fias Publishing, 2011)
[60] Ibid. p. 13

scrupulous with minimal significant variations. The reliability of transmission of the Old Testament has been substantiated.

3. The plethora of New Testament manuscripts (5,686[61]) and fragments (over 25,000) allows us to get extremely close to the text of the autographs. The reliability of the transmission of the New Testament has been substantiated.

4. The historical and geographical information claimed in the Bible has been proved to be remarkably accurate where such corroborative information exists from archaeology and extrabiblical documentation. Such information affirms the reliability of the biblical text.

5. While we have limited extrabiblical knowledge of circumstances before the United Monarchy period of Israel (Saul, David, and Solomon), what we do have largely authenticates what is written in the Bible.

In the cases where the historical record seems to verify or discredit the Bible, by a wide majority we can verify that the Bible is true. Each text of the Bible must be weighed on its own, a project far greater than the work of this book can manage. And while the world is full of detractors, skeptics and minimalists, there is also a large body of biblical scholars who affirm the historicity, accuracy, and reliability of the Bible both in general and in many specifics.

What cannot be confirmed by scientific or historical research are the miracles of the Bible, except for the resurrection itself. The miracles of the Old Testament and of Jesus are like rocks tossed in a pond: they create a noticeable but not a lasting or repeatable effect. In the same sense that I cannot prove to you what I was thinking a minute ago, no one can prove by the science lab that Elijah parted the Jordan, that a pillar of cloud and fire accompanied the Israelites, or that an axe head floated. But because I cannot prove to you that I threw a pebble into a stream doesn't mean it didn't happen, and while one may insist that extraordinary claims require extraordinary evidence, such evidence cannot possibly be produced when events, such as my thoughts, produce no evidential material. A criterion different from material evidence is called for in the case of effects that leave no

---

[61] According to the Christian Apologetics and Research Ministry

material evidence, such as the wind stinging my eyes today, or my seeing a rare bird on a branch just before it flew away. In the case of miracles, we evaluate their truth or falsity on the testimony of those who were there to record it. Whether or not we believe them rides on our assessment of the reliability of their other writings and our experiences with similar spiritual realities.

THE ALLEGED CONTRADICTIONS OF SCRIPTURE

The alleged "contradictions of Scripture" is mostly a farcical superficial reading of texts by people who haven't done their homework. The Skeptics' Annotated Bible and the hundreds (if not thousands) of websites devoted to the subject of biblical contradictions are largely lacking in research, understanding, and substance. While each text must be addressed on a case-by-case basis, the "contradictions of Scripture" is mostly a nonissue.

The accusation of biblical contradictions is very deceptive. On a casual reading, there appear to be contradictions from cover to cover in the Bible: terms, names, geography, legislation, customs, and commands. In reality, knowledge about the Bible can resolve more than 99% of them quickly, easily, and reliably.

The most common accusation about biblical contradictions comes in the Gospels where the accounts do not line up exactly. The Gospel accounts were not written to be historical documents alone. Each has a unique theological perspective to make.

Consider the reasons for their differences and the advantages of these variations.

1. If the Gospels were identical, there would be no need for four of them, but only one. We would be deprived of the different perspectives that different personalities with different reasons for writing bring to us. Because people see things differently, the only way to get an accurate picture of what happened, or what a person is like, is by talking to a variety of people who give us different nuances and characteristics. Any investigator

knows that no two eyewitness testimonies are going to agree exactly, and that if they did, it reduces the amount of information available.

2. In the rhetorical oral culture of 1st-century Palestine, stories were rehearsed orally before groups of listeners. Variation was allowed of certain characteristics of the story, but the core must remain solid and certain. Details could change as long as the flow and the point were the same. These were accepted characteristics of storytelling and do not undermine the authority or integrity of the text. We do the same thing when we tell stories or jokes. It may be slightly different each time, but it's still the same story. And someone else may tell a joke slightly differently than we do, but that doesn't matter. The joke scores its point. So also with the Gospels. Though in one rendition Jesus is going into Jericho and in another he is coming out, the blind Bartimaeus pleads for healing and receives it.

As another example, in the book of Acts, Luke records three times for us the account of the conversion of Paul. All three accounts are different. It is obvious that variation in the telling was both common and expected without compromising the integrity of the text.

3. The variations of the Gospel accounts prove that their writing was not based on collusion or conspiracy, but four individuals giving independent accounts of Jesus' ministry. It actually strengthens the integrity of the text that they are telling the same story in different words with different personalities.

4. Jesus taught primarily in Aramaic (though he most likely could also speak Greek and possibly Latin). Therefore, the Gospels record for us very few of the actual "words" of Jesus, for his words in the Gospels are written in Greek. Therefore, His words have been already translated. It's understandable that there are going to be slight variations in how each author translates his Aramaic into the Greek of "what Jesus said".

5. Even today we can pick up in the bookstore various biographies of President Abraham Lincoln. Those biographies differ from each other in the events they report, which they omit, and in the purpose for which they are assembled into the book.

There is no reason to believe they contradict each other, or that they are all false. Their differences actually give us a broader picture of Lincoln. It is no different with the Gospels.

If any of us today were to write a book on "What America is Like," each of those books would be different. We would choose different historical events, news events, and cultural events to emphasize, to the neglect of others. We would expect treatises on American culture to vary depending on the writer and his perspective. It is no problem that the accounts don't line up exactly; it doesn't prove them to be false. No one can capture all of American culture, Abraham Lincoln, or Jesus in one volume.

Let's look at a few examples to give you the idea.

There are different accounts about the empty tomb. Each of the Gospels tells a different story, and critics often yell "Foul! They contradict each other!" First we must recognize that none of the Gospels tells the full story, but only the pieces that pertain to each writer's agenda. We have to try to piece together the whole puzzle, which is where it can get tricky. So here is possibly how it went down: Jesus is buried in the tomb of Joseph, while some of the women watch. The tomb is sealed, and a guard is posted, probably some time during the day on Saturday. On Sunday morning, at least 3 women (possibly more) go to the tomb to finish anointing the body (some of the Gospel writers mention just one of the women, and others more). The women arrive at the tomb at dawn and are shocked to see it is empty. Mary Magdalene runs to tell the disciples, leaving the other women behind. The women still at the tomb see two angels, who tell them Jesus has risen, and to go tell the disciples to meet him in Galilee. They leave the scene but don't tell anyone. The guards rouse, and leave the scene to report the empty tomb to the authorities.

Mary Magdalene, meanwhile, has told Peter and John, who run to the tomb. John looks in, Peter bursts in, then John follows him in. They leave the scene.

Mary Magdalene then returns to the tomb, still very upset. She sees the angels in a different position than they previously had been, and then sees Jesus, who speaks with her. She is reassured and convinced. Then she leaves the scene.

Later that day Jesus appears to Peter, and then the story continues on from there.

What about the rooster crow? Matthew, Luke, & John say the rooster would crow once after Peter's denial, and Mark says twice. Anyone who has ever slept in a rural part of a foreign country knows that the roosters crow through the night with barely a break. Wearing earplugs is almost a must for we Westerners, dealing with the dogs barking and roosters crowing what seems to be all night long. Jesus' point is not to count the number of crows, but to say that before morning Peter will have denied him three times. Here's a plausible scenario: After Peter denied Christ for the 3rd time, a rooster crowed twice in quick succession, a distinct reminder to Peter of Jesus' words. Thus Matthew, Luke, and John are right: Immediately after Peter's 3rd denial, the rooster did crow. Mark adds an additional detail, probably coming from the story told to him by Peter himself: It didn't just crow, but twice in a row, a poignant symbol and painful reminder of what Jesus had said. Both could easily be true.

Do we have Jesus' exact words? No. First of all, Jesus spoke in Aramaic, and the Gospels are written in Greek. What did Jesus *actually* say? Most likely he said, "Before the rooster crows twice." Matthew, Luke, and John know that what was important is that the rooster crowed immediately after Peter's denial, and so they give the condensed version: "Before the rooster crows, you'll deny me three times." There was nothing inaccurate or incorrect about it. It's like me telling one person "I'm going to see a movie at 9:30, and I'll stay for the midnight showing of another." But I tell another friend, "I'm going to go see a movie." The second one is neither a lie nor a contradiction. Or if I told someone I was going to go see two movies back to back tonight–a double feature, and then that person told one person I was going to see two movies and another person, in a different context, that I went to see a movie last night (which is true). This is not a problem in real life. We do it all the time.

What about Jesus' last words from the cross? The Gospels tell the story differently. Again, each Gospel writer includes what suits his theme in writing. Jesus spoke seven sentences from the cross, and no Gospel writer records them all. We don't know which line was actually last, and it doesn't much matter. The sentences Luke and John relate (different sentences) could have been spoken closely to each other in quick succession, and each writer just picks one to tell about. Some think Jesus' dying words from the cross would have been remembered more vividly. Remember that few disciples were there, mostly a few women, Jesus' mother Mary, and John. Possibly the "Into your hands I commit my spirit" struck Mary to the heart, and she communicated them to Luke when he interviewed her. John himself was there, and the "IT IS FINISHED" fits so well into the point of his Gospel that's what he includes.

In all of these, no one Gospel writer is writing everything. They pick and choose, and they're allowed to. If I took you to a busy scene, and told you to write everything—EVERYTHING—that happened for the next 6 hours, you wouldn't be able to do it. You have to pick and choose. Certain things would catch your eye and ear, and different things would catch a different writer's attention. It doesn't mean the two accounts contradict.

Who was the father of Joseph in Jesus' genealogies? First of all I have to say that genealogies in the ancient world were never supposed to include every generation. They included what fit their purposes, and didn't mind leaving gaps. Both Gospels claim to be giving Joseph's line. There are several theories about the divergent genealogies of Jesus in Matthew and Luke:

1. Matthew gives Joseph's line, and Luke gives Mary's.
2. Matthew gives Mary's line, and Luke gives Joseph's.
3. Matthew follows Jesus' natural descent through Joseph, and Luke follows Jesus' legal descent through Joseph.
4. Joseph's biological father died, and so his brother married the widow, as per levirate marriage. The two Gospels trace both lines, so no matter which way you go, Jesus comes out as a descendant of David.
5. Matthew's genealogy is through Joseph's mother, and Luke's is through Joseph's father.

It hasn't been resolved, and it may never be, but some of these are reasonable explanations that could be so. At this point no one knows, but it's not necessarily a contradiction.

What color robe was put on Jesus during his torment at the hands of the soldiers before his crucifixion? One Gospel says purple, and another says scarlet. I know I get confused sometimes whether fuchsia is a version of purple or of pink. It could go either way depending on the exact shade and the light on it. One man's scarlet is another man's purple. This is a tiny issue. The writer names the color as he perceived it. Was it reddish purple, or purplish red? We don't know, but we get the idea. It was the color of royalty. It may have even been a faded garment that had been passed along. Maybe John said purple because that's what it was made to be, but Matthew said scarlet because that's what it had turned into. And remember, it was during the night and in torchlight. Colors aren't so clear in that setting.

All of these inconsistencies are easily brushed away when we put the situations in real life. If we take them as isolated literary pieces, we diagnose each word and find room to criticize. But in the real life situation, there's a lot more going on that makes the details more fluid. What is helpful is just a little bit of research, and then putting yourself back into the situation as realistically as you can. That's usually all it takes. Often times both can be true, depending on one's vantage point. The truth of eyewitness situations is often far more complex than the narrative version of it, and inconsistencies quickly fade in the face of reality.

EVIDENCES OF DIVINE AUTHORSHIP

Someone may argue that even if the authorship of the various Bible books can be settled, even if the text itself can be proved to be reliable, and even if alleged contradictions can be explained, those are still insufficient to claim divine authorship and inspiration. On what bases can we assert that God is the author of the Bible?

1. The inner consistency of theme and teaching is unearthly. More than 40 authors from three continents, from all walks of life, spanning 1500 years have written a collection

of books that ply the same waters in the same direction, focusing concordantly on the same theme despite disparate personalities and divergent cultural backgrounds. Progression of thought and revelation as well as diversified perspectives still don't disrupt the flow of the crucial themes of the Bible: The problem of sin, the problem of a correct view of God, God's presence, God's covenant, redemption and resurrection. Their accord is so abnormal and against the odds that it can be considered extraordinarily authored.

2. Historical accuracy. We would expect a divine text to not make historical errors. The historical, geographical, and cultural information in the Bible has been proved to be remarkably accurate where corroborative information exists.

3. Fulfilled prophecy. The Bible is full of fulfilled prophecy, from predictions about a few days down the road to ones centuries in the future.

4. Many converts to Christianity speak of how their lives have been changed in ways that are unparalleled in any other religious system, political posturing, psychological enlightenment, or optimistic philosophy. The way the lives of people who become Christians are changed is radically different from converts to other religions. Other religious recruits don new clothes and take on some new habits to conform to their new faith, and they speak of renewed purpose or peace in life. But people who turn to Christ speak of the "loads of life being lifted," of entirely new demeanors and personalities overcoming them, of miraculous changes in life (give up alcohol, done with drugs, etc.), and of radical life change in attitude and behavior. The record stands throughout history that the life change caused by Christian commitment is unique.

5. There is little reasonable explanation, other than the action of God, for the perpetuation of the Jewish nation and the origin and continuance of the Church (see point #6). Every other ancient society of the Middle East except Egypt (Assyrians, Babylonians, Sumerians, Edomites, Hittites, Philistines, Ammonites, etc.) has crumbled through time, but even Egypt

lasted because they had a land to maintain their identity. The Jews only had a nation to call their own for about 400 years, after which time they were dispersed to the four winds, just like every other nation that was battered by the ancient empires. Despite being conquered and dispersed, having no homeland for thousands of years, and with concerted attempts to eradicate them from the globe, they and their writings continue on. The survival of the Jewish nation gives credence to an explanation of divine action, which is exactly what the Bible claims and is one of its main narratives. The survival of the Jews gives another point of evidence that God is at work in the writing of history and His record of it in the Bible.

6. As far as the Church is concerned, observe the radical change of Jewish stalwarts of the first century to a dedicated group of Christians who no longer follow the ceremonial law, perform the sacrifices, or recognize the Temple. For so many, who were so dedicated to their stringent faith, to depart so radically en masse betrays that they were unreservedly convinced that a man actually came back from the dead and it changed all of their lives and history forever. They did not interpret their Scriptures to be speaking of a crucified and resurrected Messiah, and yet they came to believe and proclaim that such was the case. We have their story in the New Testament.

7. The sensibleness of the Bible. It is a literary treasure of God revealing himself, amply filled with wisdom, life guidance, a harmony of theme and thought, speaking to real life, and addressing the human condition with honesty and hope. There's no book or power like it.

For Further Reading:

John Walton and D. Brent Sandy, <u>The Lost World of Scripture</u>
Craig Evans, <u>God Speaks</u>
Craig Blomberg, <u>Can We Still Believe the Bible?</u>

CHAPTER THREE
THE CONUNDRUM OF JESUS

The question Jesus asked of his disciples still stands like Gibraltar overlooking the ocean of humanity: "Who do you say I am?" (Mark 8.29). Answers still run the gamut from demonic through deranged, "he was a good man," "he was a prophet," and all the way to "he was divine," as they did then. Recently another opinion has been added: He never existed. "Jesus is fictional." Almost everything we know about Jesus appears in the Bible; he is relatively unknown in contemporary history, a fact that fuels the skepticism of detractors. "Surely," they muse, "a man who did such marvelous and miraculous things would have attracted the attention of *somebody* who would have recorded *something* about him." They feel the silence is deafening. The claim is that the Roman world of the 1st century is one of the most well recorded eras in ancient history, and yet there is almost *nothing* to corroborate the Gospel narratives about Jesus. Yet simultaneously Christians regard Jesus as the very fulcrum of history, the man on whose lifetime and eternity balances and turns. Who was this enigmatic, magnificent, challenging, "non-existent", wise, misunderstood, miracle-working, worshiped, murdered, resurrected individual? And how do we know?

THE QUESTION OF HISTORICITY

Before we do anything else it behooves us to try to ascertain whether Jesus was real or a legend. For unbelievers it's not a particularly important question and apathy is common, but for Christians, Jesus' historicity is paramount. Christian theology requires Jesus' historicity; if Jesus did not actually live as a human, then redemption for our sins never happened, blood was never spilled, resurrection is not a reality, and the Christian faith is worthless (1 Corinthians 15:17-19). It matters.

Aside from the Gospel writers, Jesus is not mentioned by any eyewitness. The historical records of Josephus (the authenticity and reliability of which have been called into question) and Tacitus are both secondhand accounts. Neither of these gentlemen ever met Jesus or even saw him. They were not even alive when Jesus was. Yet their accounts, along with the Gospels, have enough truth and credibility (Tacitus is considered to be one of the greatest Roman historians) to convince the large majority of modern historians that "Jesus existed historically."[62] "[W]ith very few exceptions, ...critics do support the historicity of Jesus, and reject the theory that Jesus never existed, known as the 'Christ myth theory.'"[63] One of the citations by Josephus (*Antiquities* 20, 9,1) and the one by Tacitus (*Annals*, book 15, chapter 44) are widely regarded as reliable, and are only disputed by a small number of scholars. Historian Michael Grant wrote that "If we apply to the New Testament, as we should, the same sort of criteria as we should apply to other ancient writings containing historical material, we can no more reject Jesus' existence than we can reject the existence of a mass of pagan personages whose reality as historical figures is never questioned."[64]

Atheist Neil Carter argues for the historicity of Jesus on his blogsite:[65]

---

[62] http://en.wikipedia.org/wiki/Historicity_of_Jesus

[63] Ibid.

[64] Michael Grant, *Jesus: An Historian's Review of the Gospels*, 1977

[65] http://www.patheos.com/blogs/godlessindixie/2014/09/04/an-atheists-defense-of-the-historicity-of-jesus/

I can't believe I'm feeling the need to do this, but today I'd like to write a brief defense of the historicity of Jesus.

When climate change deniers want to insist that our actions have no impact on global temperatures, they display a remarkable disdain for an entire discipline populated by credentialed professionals in that field who say otherwise. It doesn't seem to bother the deniers that they themselves have no specialization in the academic field they disparage because in any field of study there will always be at least some small contingent who go against the consensus. The existence of those outliers is justification enough for the deniers to say, "This business is far from certain, you know. Just look at these four people who disagree!"

That's how I feel when people in the skeptic community argue that Jesus never existed. They are dismissing a large body of work for which they have insufficient appreciation, most often due to the fact that they themselves have never formally studied the subject. And yes, I know that the study of religion and of antiquity is a far 'softer' field of study than climatology (and therefore more subject to personal bias). But that doesn't mean we can't reasonably conclude anything at all about the distant past. There are at least a handful of things about the origins of the Christian religion which we can reasonably conclude based on the things that we know. Among them are that there was most likely a guy named Jesus who preached and was killed outside Jerusalem, and that after his death a diverse following emerged which built around that event a narrative which grew to become the Christian faith.

The existence of two or three professionals within the study of antiquity claiming that Jesus never existed does not signal a sea change in that field. There haven't been any new discoveries in the past few years which signal any significant changes in that discipline. The only thing I see that's changed is public opinion.

Another possible corroboration of an actual man Jesus of Nazareth comes from the now famous and hotly debated James Ossuary—a bone box with no verifiable provenance that has incised on the side of it, "James, son of Joseph, brother of Jesus." The box has been dated from 20 BC to AD 70. It has been studied in minute detail by epigraphists, professors, archaeologists, paleographers, historians, geochemists, and geologists, and has been deemed to be authentic by some,[66] a forgery by others.[67] If it's authentic, the bone box provides strong evidence for the historicity of the person we know as Jesus of Nazareth.

Nevertheless: "The increasingly common view of Jesus among New Testament scholars as of 2007 is that 'historical research can indeed disclose a core of historical facts about Jesus.' "[68]

OTHER EVIDENCES OF JESUS

We are mistaken to expect that the historicity of Jesus can only be confirmed by archaeology. Just as in chapter 1 (the evidences of God), there are evidences for the life of Jesus that have nothing to do with parchments and historically corroborative documentation. Again, I'm under no illusion (or delusion) that these "evidences" aren't able to be argued against, and skeptics will find them less than convincing, but I think all of the evidence together paints a more believable picture than merely looking at the bits and pieces. Of course it would

---

[66] It has been declared authentic by Amnon Rosenfeld (emeritus geophysicist with the Geological Survey of Israel), Shimon Ilane (geophysicist with the Geological Survey of Israel), André Lemaire (paleographer at the Sorbonne), Edward Keal and Ewa Dziadowiec (curator and conservator, respectively, of the Royal Ontario Museum in Toronto, Joseph Fitzmyer (Aramaicist), Ada Yardeni (the leading Israeli authority on Hebrew and Aramaic script), Wolfgang Krumbein (Carl von Ossietzky University in Oldenburg, Germany), James Herrell (University of Toledo)

[67] The Israeli Antiquities Authority published a report in 2003 concluding that it was a fake. The defendants in the "forgery trial of the century" were subsequently acquitted, not convicted.

[68] http://rationalwiki.org/wiki/Evidence_for_the_historical_ existence_of_Jesus_Christ

be helpful for historians to find many local contemporaneous authors reporting about the wonderful miracle worker from Galilee, but that obviously has not happened, and yet Jesus is considered by most to be a historical person. What else gives his historicity credibility?

Christianity as a Faith System

Out of seemingly nowhere, in about AD 30, a new and vibrant belief system upended one of the most well-established religious systems of history (Judaism), in its very own holy capital city, by abolishing the majority of its most valued practices (the ceremonial law and sacrifices). The existence of Christianity constitutes a strong evidence that a man named Jesus radically changed the lives of his followers. Judaism was (and is) one of the strongest of entrenched religious practices that ever developed on earth. Right in the hotbed of Judaism, in Jerusalem in the 1st century, the most reasonable explanation for the rise of Christianity is the presence, teaching, death, and resurrection of Jesus. John and Peter, in their New Testament writings, both claim that they base what they are writing and teaching on the reality that they saw, touched, and heard Jesus (1 John 1.1-3; 2 Peter 1.16-18). A reasonable explanation of the rise of Christianity in the capital of Judaism is the historical reality of the historical Jesus.

Life Change in the Apostles

What would motivate a moderately-sized group of thoroughly Jewish men suddenly to follow another teaching? I might ask an analogous question: What would it take to convert thousands of Muslims who live in Mecca suddenly to become Hindus, all in a relatively short amount of time? What it would take would be something real and dramatic happening that convinced them beyond a reasonable doubt that there was a truth higher than the religion to which they already subscribed. That's a major obstacle, but the fact that it happened in Jerusalem in the middle of the 1st century gives credibility to the historicity of a man named Jesus who so influenced a large group of stalwart Jews that they made an overnight change. They didn't just change religions, their lives were radically changed.

THE QUESTION OF MIRACLES

Atheists pose the questions and offer opinions:

"What is the proof of God and Jesus committing miracles?"

"I don't believe miracles are possible. Walking on water and multiplying bread are common magic tricks performed by various stage magicians."

"Miracles just don't make sense to me. They don't square with science and they don't fit with reason. It just has to be that they were made up to enhance the story."

Skeptics want hard and direct evidence that can be dug up by archaeologists, or indisputable writings corroborated by other reliable written sources, or at the very least scientific evidence that the miracle was reasonably possible in a natural world. They also claim that the Gospels are demonstrably false because of its mention of miracles. All of these are using an inappropriate measuring system for the object at hand.

The miracles of the Bible are more like pebbles dropped in a stream than they are like pottery hidden in the soil. There is no lasting effect and no possible proof for later generations to find. If it's true that Jesus walked on the water, what artifact do you expect an archaeologist to dig up, or writings from anyone other than the twelve who saw it? In our courts of law, if twelve witnesses confirmed an event, a jury would give strength to that unanimity of testimony. But more to the point is: Does the lack of lasting evidence prove it didn't happen?

The way science generally works is that a hypothesis is stated and an experiment is designed to test the hypothesis. Depending on the hypothesis, specimens are gathered or facts are measured and repeated and documented. Through trial and error the technique and instrumentation necessary are refined to give the information desired, and patterns are established to help eliminate spurious ideas (or specimens) and measuring mistakes. HOW IS ANY OF THIS POSSIBLE IN THE EVENT OF A SPONTANEOUS MIRACLE?

Suppose I were hiking a trail in Vermont with some friends, and the five of us saw a catamount (cougar; mountain lion) cross the path in front of us. He was there and gone so quickly that none of us was able to take a picture. When we go back to the house eager to tell our story, other family members may want to see the evidence. We have none, but we each saw it and testify to it. We tell other friends, and they check on the Internet and discover that scientists say there haven't been catamounts in Vermont in decades. Does that mean we didn't see one?

What enduring evidence does one expect of the feeding of the 5,000, walking on the water, or Jesus healing a lame man? Certainly nothing an archaeologist can find, and obviously not a phenomenon a scientist can test and confirm. Asking for scientific proof of Jesus' miracles is like asking a doctor to use a stethoscope to verify that I had a bout with hiccups last week.

Much more important to the discussion of miracles is the identity claims that Jesus made. Jesus claimed that the miracles he performed were signs of his deity. If there is no such thing as God, we would expect miracles to be a ridiculous imaginative mistake that people make based on wishful thinking or legend building. But if God is a real being, miracles are no problem. Indubitably, the Creator God, having been the designer and creator of the laws of physics, has the freedom and power to use those laws or supersede them at his desire and to serve his purposes.

If there is such a being as God, and if Jesus was his incarnation on earth, it would not at all be improbable for God to empower him to do miraculous signs. The question is more the identity of Jesus than the rationality of miracles by his hand.

Alvin Plantinga[69] asks what the problem is in believing in miracles—why should anyone object to it? "Why can't the causal continuum be rent by the interference of supernatural, transcendent powers? Why are miracles necessarily incompatible with modern science? They are only incompatible if it can be proved that nature is a closed continuum of cause and effect, and closed to intervention or interference on the part of beings outside that continuum, including God himself."[66] In no way does the predictable character of nature exclude the possibility of miraculous events. Science cannot prove that

---

[69] Alvin Plantinga, Where the Conflict Really Lies: Science, Religion, & Naturalism, (New York, NY: Oxford University Press, 2011), pp. 71-119

[66] Ibid. p. 72

[67] Ibid. p. 82

the universe is all there is, meaning that it's a closed causal system. "Natural laws offer no threat to special divine action."[67]

The only way to show that miracles are impossible is to disprove the existence of God, a task that is both logically and scientifically impossible.

THE EVIDENCE OF JESUS' MIRACLES

- The records of the Gospel writers were still within the lifetime of the people who had been there. Such reporting could easily still be confirmed or debunked. If the tales were easily able to be discredited, it would have made them all look like fools.
- Jesus' miracles were one of the major evidences to convince them that he was who he claimed to be. His healing, the Transfiguration, and his resurrection were a large part of what motivated them to accept that he was God. Their faith was based in part on the miraculous signs they saw him perform.
- The inclusion of verifiable historical data in the miracle stories lends credibility to the entire narrative. When Peter drew his sword and chopped off Malchus's ear in the Garden of Gethsemane, Jesus heals the man on the spot (John 18.10). The verifiable data is given: His name is Malchus, he works for Caiaphas, and it was his ear that was injured. These details are given so the story could be verified as historically accurate. The authors obviously intended their accounts of the miracles to be interpreted as historical events.
- Josephus, in a text considered to be historically reliable, mentions "Jesus, a wise man. For he was one who did surprising deeds..."[70]
- The cultural milieu of Jesus' life speaks to the truthfulness of the record. The era of 1st-century Palestine was not one characterized by superstition and gullibility. Jews were educated people, and Romans and Greeks were skeptics. That the Gospels record that people swarmed around Jesus, both requesting and experiencing miracles, is evidence of

---

[70] Josephus, *Antiquities* (Book 18), the *Testimonium Flavianum*

their veracity. What is also often recorded is that the people were skeptical of Jesus' ability to do miracles until they saw with their own eyes and were convinced. What is lacking is corroborative writing other than the written record of Jesus' miracles is in the Bible itself.

- Jesus' enemies even admitted that he performed miracles (Matthew 12.22-24; 14.54-57; John 3.2).
- Alternative interpretations of the miracles (mass hallucinations, mythical creations of biased authors, etc.) lack credibility upon examination. There is no such thing as mass hallucination, and the historical nature of the narratives, along with the intent of the authors to have been recording history speaks strongly against alternative interpretations.
- The resurrection of Jesus is immensely compelling (as explained below).[71]

THE QUESTION OF THE RESURRECTION

Every true Christian understands or acknowledges that everything we believe hangs on a literal, physical resurrection of Jesus. If it did not happen, our faith is worthless (1 Corinthians 15.14). If it did happen, it verifies Jesus' claims to deity and the truth of his teachings. According to Christians, everything we believe hinges on the fulcrum of Jesus' physical and literal resurrection. If he truly rose from the dead, it has tremendous and undeniable import for every human being, and for the meaning of life and the reality of the afterlife.

There were no eyewitnesses that we know of to the resurrection event itself in real time. All of the eyewitness testimony we have comes at sunrise and afterwards. How do we know Jesus rose from the dead?

- The empty tomb. All four Gospels mention the empty tomb.[72]
  ▷ Not a single ancient writer, Christian or secular, refutes the fact that the tomb was empty.

---

[71] Lanier, Op cit., p. 207
[72] Matthew 28.6; Mark 16.6; Luke 24.3; John 20.1-2.

▷ The tomb of Christ was a known locale. Any claims could be conveniently verified. It was a location known to both friends and enemies: believers, Romans, and Jews. The disciples could not have credibly preached the resurrection in Jerusalem if Jesus' body was still in the tomb. No one ever produced a dead body. Jesus was publicly executed and publicly buried. Christianity would not have flourished in Jerusalem if someone could just say, "Here's the dead body of Jesus."

▷ There would be no claim that the body had been stolen if the body were still in the tomb.

• The narrative is being told by eyewitnesses

▷ The disciples made repeated claims that they saw the risen Jesus with their own eyes.

▷ John 20.1, 5, 6, & 8 use the word "saw."

• The stone was rolled away from the entrance of the tomb.

▷ The stone probably weighed several thousand pounds.[73] Four round ones have been found in and around Jerusalem.[74]

▷ It took more than one person to move these heavy stones (John 11.41). Since the tomb was heavily guarded, a group sneaking in to move the stone is highly improbable.

▷ The rock-hewn tombs were usually closed by a large circular stone, set in a slanting groove so that when the stone was released, it would by its own weight and the force of gravity roll into place over the door. Very little strength would be required to close the door, but the united effort of several men would be necessary to open it. Since the stone was found rolled away, or lifted out of its track, it must have been moved by some powerful force and for a definite purpose.[75]

---

[73] Oliver Greene, *The Gospel According to John* (The Gospel Hour, Inc., 1966) p. 326

[74] Amos Kloner, "Did A Rolling Stone Close Jesus' Tomb?, *Biblical Archaeology Review,* Sept/Oct 1999, pp. 23ff

[75] Merrill Tenney, *John: The Gospel of Belief* (Grand Rapids, MI: William B. Eerdmans Publishing Co., 1948), p. 280

[74] Ibid., p. 280

▷ The women had not expected to find it rolled away, and were incapable of moving it themselves. The disciples would not have moved it, or they would have no reasons to run that morning to see what had happened. The enemies of Jesus were not responsible, for it was wholly to their interest to keep the body where it was. John gives the impression that it was done by divine intervention.[74]

▷ John uses a term implying violence, that the stone was lifted out of the groove in which it ran.[76]

• The grave clothes were in their place, with the head cloth folded separately.

▷ If the body had been stolen, these clothes would have been stolen with it.

▷ No robber would take the time to neatly fold a head cloth and leave it in a decorative position.

▷ The description of the grave clothes and head cloth seem to be that they were still in the same position as when the body was present, as if the body had risen straight out of the wrappings.[77]

• Jesus was seen by credible witnesses after his crucifixion and resurrection.

▷ Mary Magdalene, when she was alone (John 20.14)

▷ Certain women returning from the tomb (Matthew 28.8-10)

▷ Peter, when he was alone (Luke 24.34)

▷ Two disciples on the road to Emmaus (Luke 24.13-16)

▷ Ten apostles in Jerusalem, without Thomas (John 20.19-24)—certainly an odd event if the narrative is fictional.

▷ Eleven apostles in Jerusalem, this time with Thomas (John 20.26)

▷ Seven disciples fishing in the Sea of Galilee (John 21.1, 2)

▷ Eleven apostles (and possibly others) on a mountain in Galilee (Matthew 28.16-20)

[76] Leon Morris, *The Gospel According to John* (Grand Rapids, MI: William B. Eerdmans Publishing Co., 1995) p. 734 note 10

[77] Craig Keener, The IVP Bible Background Commentary: New Testament, (Downers Grove, IL: InterVarsity Press) p. 316

> ▷ More than 500 people at one time (1 Corinthians 15.6). There is no such thing as a mass (group) hallucination.
> ▷ James, when he was alone (1 Corinthians 15.7)
> ▷ Eleven apostles on the Mount of Olives, at his ascension (Acts 1.1-12)

- The apostles were not expecting the resurrection, they did not understand Jesus' teachings, and there is no reasonable explanation why they would have made up something so unnatural. They had nothing to gain from circulating a wild and fabricated story. In an honor and shame culture as was the Jewish world of the 1st century Roman Empire, it would make no sense to create a story of a man crucified in such a shameful way by Rome who had miraculously risen again unless they really believed it to be authentically and historically true.[78] Even the idea was sheer madness to both Jews and Gentiles.
- The story of the resurrection circulated extremely quickly after Jesus' death. If it were fictional, all anyone had to do was retrieve the dead body as evidence. And, like today, who would even believe it unless it was from a known, credible, and reliable source? The earliest reports of the resurrection are so close to the event itself that it's unreasonable to assume it was merely a legend that developed. Scholars of both Christian and non-Christian persuasion have dated the creed of 1 Corinthians 15.3-8 to within only a few years of Jesus' resurrection.
- There is no credible evidence that the apostles were anything other than sane, sincere, and reliable men.
- Men are generally not willing to die for a known lie. Even if one person is, eleven aren't. The stories of history we have claim that all eleven disciples (or perhaps only ten) died a martyr's death. Many are willing to die for what they believe to be true, or for what they believe to be a noble cause, but they will rarely die for what they *know* to be a lie. While believing something doesn't make it true, it's not reasonable to think they would die for a questionable belief that would bring them death for treason. The evidence is that they knew without a doubt the truth of the resurrection.

---

[78] Ben Witherington III, *Biblical Archaeology Review*, Mar/Apr 2011, p. 30

- The elements of the narrative have the character of historicity: women as the first witnesses (an absurdity in Jewish culture—women were not allowed to testify in court), the apostles deserting Jesus, two unnamed disciples on the road to Emmaus as eyewitnesses—all of these are ridiculous claims that hurt their case unless it actually happened this way.
- As mentioned previously, a literal and historical resurrection is the most reasonable conclusion to explain why many stalwart 1st-century Jews would abandon the Sabbath, the sacrifices, and the Law of Moses and claim the reality of a physical resurrection in the city in which it recently occurred. If the story were false, it would be quickly and easily stamped out.
- The idea of an immediate bodily resurrection return to earthly life was not part of their culture, not Greek, Roman, or any part of Judaism.[79] There is a unified, precise, articular and confident belief in a physical and bodily resurrection from the dead back to human life as a unique affirmation. There is no cultural context for such an assertion. Jesus' resurrection accounts for both the strong similarity between Christianity and Judaism and equally clear dissimilarities. Early Christianity was a resurrection movement.
- Conspiracy theories about the disciples don't hold water.
  - ▷ Eleven conspirators are easy to crack. There are too many variables for the conspiracy to hold together.
  - ▷ Conspirators separated by miles and non-communication quickly manufacture different accounts.
  - ▷ Conspirators who are not particularly friends, as the disciples weren't, won't lie and die for each other.
  - ▷ Conspirators with nothing to gain but persecution and death will not hold the conspiracy together.
- Claims that they all went to the wrong tomb are not believable
  - ▷ The Jewish leaders had every motivation to correct their mistake and produce the dead body of Jesus.
  - ▷ When Peter and John ran to the tomb to verify Mary's story, they certainly would have recognized her error and

---

[79] N.T. Wright, The Resurrection of the Son of God (Minneapolis, MN: Fortress Press, 2003) p. 210

corrected it.

▷ The wrong tomb would not likely have had grave clothes in it.

• Claims that the body was stolen don't make sense.

▷ The disciples were not expecting a resurrection. They would not likely have perpetrated the deceitful scheme.

▷ The disciples were in fear for their own lives, and were in hiding. They would not have attacked the guard posted at the tomb.

▷ The tomb was guarded by Roman soldiers, and intrusion could easily mean death to the perpetrators.

▷ The Jews had no motive to steal the body. But if they had stolen it to prevent specious claims of resurrection, they could have produced the body after the rumors began to squelch them.

▷ The Romans had no motive to steal the body. A cadre of Roman soldiers was assigned to guard the tomb to *prevent* problems and rumors. A claim of resurrection would have thrown the city into turmoil, and the Romans wanted to prevent that.

▷ If friends had stolen the body, they would likely have taken the precious, blood-stained cloth, still covering the honored corpse, with them.[80]

▷ There were no valuables buried with him on Friday. There is no motive for a thief to break into the tomb.

▷ It's not reasonable to think that someone would steal the body but leave behind the graveclothes and neatly fold the head cloth separately.

• Claims that the disciples were delusional are not reasonable.

▷ There is no such thing as group hallucinations.

▷ After the resurrection, the disciples wrote sane and logical treatises.

▷ All that was necessary to prove they were delusional would be to produce a body, which was never done.

▷ The Old Testament Scriptures are filled with themes and stories of resurrection (Enoch, Noah and the flood, Isaac

---

[80] Arthur Pink, *Exposition of the Gospel of John*
(I.C. Herendeen Swengel: PA, 1945) p.

[Genesis 22], Israel out of Egypt, etc.). Resurrection is consistent with biblical teaching and expectations. John 2.2 (repeated by the angels in Luke 24.6) tells us that Jesus had referred to these during his ministry. The first response of the disciples and the women had been that the body must have been stolen, not that Jesus had risen. Only when the angels remind them about Jesus' words and the Old Testament Scriptures, in conjunction with meeting Jesus himself, do they finally understand his teachings about death and resurrection, and are convinced of the truth of His resurrection.

Since our desire is to infer the most reasonable conclusion, the evidence for the resurrection gives us valid reason to conclude that the unbelievable and unnatural actually happened: Jesus rose from the dead. And if the resurrection happened, that would be decisive evidence that miracles *are* possible and that the identity claims of Jesus *are* true, all of which would lead us reasonably to conclude that there is no coherent reason to doubt the possibility that the other miracles of Jesus also happened and that Jesus is who he claimed to be: God in the flesh.

For Further Reading:

Alvin Plantinga, God and Other Minds
Mike Licona, The Resurrection of Jesus
N.T. Wright, The Resurrection of the Son of God
C.S. Lewis, Miracles

CHAPTER FOUR
DEFENDING THE FAITH

ACCUSATION: GOD IS EVIL BECAUSE HE IS GUILTY OF GENOCIDE.

The accusation is that several times (under Moses, Joshua, and King Saul), God ordered the extermination of the Canaanites and the Amalekites. The accusations are as follows:

"Assuming that man has an innate sense that killing infants is wrong, what would you expect to see as a reaction from a nation directed by God to slaughter every living thing in the cities they attack?"

"Why did God kill the Canaanites? It sure seems that God is a murderer, guilty of ethnic cleansing. How can a loving God order people killed? How can you worship such a violent, vicious God?"

Let me first lay some groundwork, and then I'll speak more specifically.

1. The only time(s) that the Israelites were commanded by God to fight offensive battles (to conquer cities and take the land) was during the conquest of Canaan under Joshua. Beyond the land of Canaan, they were *never* commanded

to expand their boundaries, build an empire, or wipe out people groups.

2. The goal of the conquest was not genocide, but occupation. Repeatedly the commands of God are to drive the Canaanites from the land (Exodus 23.30 is one example of many). More to the point, the Canaanites were first to be given an opportunity to surrender and become part of Israel (Deuteronomy 20.10), and if they would not surrender, only then were the Israelites to engage them in battle.

3. It was God's intent all along to bless all the nations (Genesis 12.3 and others). It's not the Canaanites as people that the Lord finds intolerable, but their godless perversions and false religion. Deuteronomy 7.5-6 is very clear that the point is truth, not genocide.

4. In those days the cities were fortresses surrounding governmental and cultic structures, not dwellings for the population. When commands were given to conquer cities, it was the rulers and soldiers the army was after, not the population. In the agrarian society of the Canaanite city-states, more than 90% of the people lived in the countryside as farmers, and less than 10% of the population lived in the cities. The cities were mostly fortresses and political centers, not large enough to house or protect a population within its walls. Almost exclusively, when a city was attacked, it was military action against military personnel and the rulers of the region, not against the general (and innocent) population. It was impossible to wipe out all the citizenry, and there was never an attempt to do so.

5. The Conquest of Joshua is not what many people imagine. Joshua cut a strategic line through the center of Canaan by conquering Jericho, Ai and Shechem (Joshua 6-9), separating the north of Canaan from the south. The city of Gibeah surrendered (Josh. 9), and they were not killed. At that point an alliance of cities from the south attacked Joshua's forces (Josh. 10), and the Israelites won. Now they controlled the southern hill country. Joshua then turned and attacked one city, Hazor, in the north and burned it (Josh.

11), and an alliance of northern cities subsequently attacked him. Joshua won, and all of the hill country of Canaan was now in Israelite hands. That was the extent of it (Josh 11.16, 23, etc.). In other words, only four of the battles the Israelites fought during the conquest were offensive. The Israelites never gained the valleys and plains until under the monarchy, at which time local nation-states attacked David and he won. There *was* no genocide.

Now let's talk about ancient Near-Eastern warfare. The "kill 'em all" speeches of the ancient Near East were a case of customary warfare bravado, and people in those days didn't take it literally. What it meant was: "Secure a total victory." The language is used in Josh. 10.40-42; 11.16-23; yet they readily acknowledge that it wasn't literally true (Judges 1.21, 27-28). On the one hand, Joshua says he utterly destroyed the Anakim (Josh. 11.21-22), but then he gives Caleb permission to drive them out of the land (Josh. 14.12-15; cf. 15.13-19). What it proves it that "kill them all" was an idiom of warfare that meant "We won a decisive victory." No people groups were being wiped out. This was pretty typical of the whole region in this era, as is evidence by the following records.

- Egypt's Thutmosis III (late 15th c.) boasted that "the numerous army of Mitanni was overthrown within the hour, annihilated totally, like those (now) not existent." In fact, Mitanni's forces lived on to fight in the 15th and 14th centuries BC.[81]
- Hittite king Mursilli II (who ruled from 1322-1295 BC) recorded making "Mt. Asharpaya empty (of humanity)" and the "mountains of Tarikarimu empty (of humanity)." Not true; just rhetoric.
- The "Bulletin" of Ramses II tells of Egypt's less-than-spectacular victories in Syria (1274 BC). Nevertheless, he announces that he slew "the entire force" of the Hittites,

---

[81] These bullet points come from Paul Copan, *Is God A Moral Monster?* (Grand Rapids, MI: Baker Books, 2011) pp. 170-172

indeed "all the chiefs of all the countries," disregarding the "millions of foreigners," which he considered "chaff."

- In the Merneptah Stele (ca. 1230 BC), Rameses II's son Merneptah announced, "Israel is wasted, his seed is not" (meaning his descendants were all killed), another premature declaration. Not true, it didn't happen, no genocide.
- Moab's king Mesha (840/830 BC) bragged that the northern kingdom of "Israel has utterly perished for always," which was over a century premature. It wasn't true. The Assyrians devastated Israel in 722 BC.
- The Assyrian ruler Sennacherib (701-681 BC) used similar hyperbole: "The soldiers of Hirimme, dangerous enemies, I cut down with the sword; and not one escaped."

In addition, we know that the people groups that Joshua claims were "utterly destroyed from the earth" continued on, such as the Anakim I have already mentioned. The same is true of the Amalekites of 1 Sam. 15 (the Amalekites were a people group for about 1000 years after being "totally destroyed"), and all of the Canaanite groups. The point was never to kill them all in a genocidal frenzy, but to win a decisive military victory over their armies and politicians, drive all rebels from the land, assimilate those who were willing, and to destroy the false religious practices that would corrupt the people of God.

The ultimate goal was that God would have a people set aside for relationship with Himself, that He could covenant with to reveal Himself to and redeem them from sin. All comers, Israeli and foreign, man and woman, slave and free, were welcome. All rebellious, wicked, and deceivers were not.

As you can see, the label "genocide" misleads. It's a modern tern that doesn't describe what was happening during the conquest under Joshua. The call to "kill 'em all" was the language of victory, not of genocide. The moral of the story is not to stop at a surface reading of these terms and assume God's immorality, but to understand their cultural language.

We are used to this kind of thing where language doesn't mean what it seems to obviously mean, but means instead what we in our culture understand. Let me explain. In many public buildings we see signs on the doors: "Please keep this door closed at all times." We know what that means. It doesn't mean keep the door closed at all times. It means after you go through the door, make sure the door closes behind you—that the door should be in a state of closed-ness when someone isn't going through it. But that's not what it says. Clearly it's not. It says in plain English that the door is never to be opened, doesn't it? If someone 3000 years from now from a different culture and a different language were to find this sign, they'd wonder why it was on a door, why the door wasn't boarded closed and sealed up, and they would "know" that no one ever went through this doorway because the sign on it clearly says that the door was never to be opened. Alas, the vagaries of language and meaning.

In front of the grocery store the other day there was a sign that says "No Standing." That's not what it means. We all know that. It means you can stop temporarily to load or unload passengers from your vehicle, but you couldn't park there even briefly to load or unload goods. But it certainly doesn't mean what it sounds like: that every individual in the vicinity must be seated. We know that, but that's not what the words say.

Then there's the "No Stopping" sign. It means you can't stop your vehicle, unless of course you're stopping to obey a traffic signal, sign, police officer, or to avoid an accident. So it doesn't mean no stopping, except when it means no stopping. We all understand. It's part of our culture.

When we use language like this, it doesn't mean we're all liars. These signs and expression are part of our culture, and we all know what they mean in our context. In the same way the rhetoric of the Conquest never meant genocide. They knew that. It's we, 3500 years later, who misunderstand it and accuse God of vicious, bloodthirsty immorality.

For another instance, look at the Amalekites of 1 Samuel 15. We can clearly tell that the Israelites did not take this literally. There was no attempt to wipe out the entire people group. You'll even notice in 1 Samuel 15.5 that specific action was taken so that innocents did *not* get caught up in the violence and killed along with the military population. If Saul is setting an ambush in a ravine, he is after a specific military target. The Amalekites were a nomadic group spread over a large geographic area. They weren't concentrated in cities, and most didn't live in cities (as I said, more than 90% of ancient populations didn't live in cities), and they certainly didn't all walk down the same path to the ravine at a specific time each day. Totally destroying the Amalekites in one battle is like thinking one can wipe out Al Qaeda or ISIS in one battle. That's not possible, because they are not concentrated in one location, and you certainly wouldn't set up an ambush in a ravine if that were your objective. The idea in 1 Samuel 15 was to punish concentrated populations of military power and regional leadership, not to destroy an entire people group. The city of Amalek (the military and government officials) was the target, and they understood that. Look at vv. 7-9: Saul conquered the city and chased the governmental leaders and the soldiers through the desert to kill them. That's what's going on here. 1 Sam. 15.12 implies that Saul accomplished his goal in one night. This tells us, again, that genocide was not the objective, the understanding, or the action. In v. 13 we hear from Saul himself: I conquered the city, killed the perpetrators, took the king captive, and scattered the people into the wilderness. Objective accomplished. All he did was conquer a small city. This is very typical through all of the ancient Near East when they used "genocidal" rhetoric. That's not what it means, just like "Please keep door closed at all times" and "No Standing."

In Deuteronomy 7, God tells the Israelites to "utterly destroy" the Canaanites. Then in the very next verse he says that after that they shouldn't make any treaties with them or intermarry with them. Wait a minute—aren't they all dead? No, there was no understanding of wiping out a people group. It just means win a significant victory, not "kill 'em all." We find out that the ultimate issue is religious (Dt. 7.5): What God wanted "utterly destroyed" was their altars, images, and sacred pillars. He wanted to wipe out the false religion, not the people group. See also Exodus 34.12-13; Dt. 12.2-3. The concern of "kill 'em all" was to purge the land of idolatry, not to commit genocide.

This is obvious over and over again. The evidence is consistent. If you get too hung up on the verbiage, you'll miss the meaning of the message in their cultural context, and that's the clue to understanding and misunderstanding the rhetoric.

The plan of God in the Conquest was a three-stepped plan, with each subsequent step only being necessary if the prior one had failed.

STEP 1: Incorporate the Canaanites into Israel as full members of the community, and worshipers of the true God, as was done with Rahab. This option was open to all. There was no reason to wait until the Day of the Lord to have the people worshiping the true God (Zechariah 14.16-20; Revelation 22, et al.). The Lord will take any who come to him; the invitation is always open, and no sincere seeker is refused. Any Canaanite who surrendered would become part of the Israelite community.

STEP 2: Lacking surrender, the object of the army was to drive the Canaanites from the land, not slaughter them (Exodus 23.30-31; 33.2; 34.11, 24; etc.). Let them go somewhere else to live, and let Israel have the land that was theirs to possess. Anyone who would leave was free to go, and any who would assimilate were free to stay.

STEP 3: If they won't surrender, don't want to join you, and refuse to leave, the only option is to engage them in battle. The land belonged to Israel, not the Canaanites. But the point was still not genocide, but to kill the soldiers, supplant the rulers, drive the populations out, and take possession of the land. The civilians were not necessarily harmed.

God communicated in the language of the culture, their typical Near-Eastern warfare rhetoric. Everyone in their era knew what it meant: Secure a total victory. We need to read the text through ancient eyes, not through modern ones of a different culture, era, and language.

ACCUSATION: GOD IS EVIL
BECAUSE HE IS GUILTY OF **INFANTICIDE**.

The accusation is that in the Genesis Flood, the tenth plague on Egypt (the death of the firstborn), and the conquest under Joshua, God not only commanded the killing of children, but killed them Himself!

"God is immoral. He uses his power to justify infanticide."

"God commands infanticide."

"God creates children, and then kills them for what their parents have done."

I'll deal with the three stories one at a time.

The Genesis Flood

There are a few questions we need answered before we can really assess the situation there.

First, we should talk about the nature of justice. A good judge treats people fairly (distributive justice). True justice, spread across the populations, distributes equally. The rich don't get privileges, the powerful don't get a free pass, and the poor don't get mistreated. That doesn't mean everyone gets treated the same, but it does mean everyone gets treated fairly. Some people may warrant different treatment, for instance, in the distribution of resources. A family of five should get more than a family of two. Situations may also differ where the need is different. Someone who is sick more often requires more medicine than someone who isn't. A good judge also takes into consideration an individual's or group's contribution. Someone who works may deserve a higher distribution than someone who doesn't. It depends.

Distributive justice isn't communism, however, where all get the same treatment, regardless of any other factors. A judge is just when he or she treats all people fairly.

Secondly, there is retributive justice: we treat people according to what they deserve. The bad person gets punished, and the good person gets rewarded. The criminal gets what he deserves. The punishment fits the crime – no more, no less.

Thirdly, a good judge takes into account various pertinent conditional factors such as motive, intent, mental state, and the presenting situation. True justice, therefore, must allow for nuance, mercy, suspended sentences, etc.

The Bible tells us God is all these things: distributing fairly, making the punishment fit the crime, and taking into account all the relevant factors. The accusation, though, is that the proof is in the pudding, and that God's pudding is rancid. Let's examine it.

What was the moral state of society at the time of Noah's flood? With no other records, the only writing we have upon which to base an opinion is that the world was intensely evil and corrupt beyond repair. The Bible says that the evil was both ubiquitous and endemic: the people were hopelessly rebellious, corrupt, and violent. We all know and have seen in our lifetimes that societies can collapse, completely breaking down into anarchy and evil. We know of times in history where the children in a particular culture were raised to be violent racists. We look at the atrocities of Somalia, ISIS, some parts of Nigeria, the genocides of Rwanda in the 1990s. Children are raised and trained as killers, men are violent and abusive, entire societies become complicit in the systemic wrongs. The Bible tells us that the world of Noah was incorrigibly corrupt, and we have no other evidence to the contrary. What would a responsible judge, seeking true justice, do in a situation like this? He would preserve the moral people (Genesis 6.9) and judge the incorrigible (Gn. 6.7). The honest question is: What was society like in the days of the flood, and was the judgment fair, even on the children? I dare say that none of us has enough information to assess the situation; all we have to go on is the Bible's appraisal, which was that society had collapsed and there was no hope of rehabilitation, even for the children.

A second question worth answering is "How many people are we talking about here?" Given that we don't know when the flood happened (it could have been at long as ten or twenty thousand years ago), it's entirely possible that the entire population of the planet was only about 5,000 human beings. In reality we may be talking about only a relatively small number of children.

Following that, what is the eternal fate of children who die? Is God actually punishing them, or is there somehow justice (in the form of mercy) in his actions? The Bible implies that children who die before any moral accountability enter heaven rather than hell.[82] If that is the case, then this "infanticide" leads to their ultimate salvation.

The Ten Plagues in Egypt

Let's move the conversation to the 10th plague: The killing of the firstborn of Egypt. The plagues were directed at the religious system of Egypt, a showdown between YHWH and their panoply of deities. For instance, the 9th plague was a plague of darkness. The Egyptians worshiped the sun god (Ra or Re), and so the plague of darkness showed their god to be powerless against YHWH. The other eight plagues were continuances of this same showdown between the false deities of Egypt and YHWH. Regarding the 10th plague, the pharaoh was considered to be a god on earth, and when he died, it was believed that he became Osiris, the god of the afterlife, the underworld, and the dead, and the god of resurrection and life. He was considered to be the grantor of all life.

After having rebuffed YHWH nine times, and having been on the losing end all nine times, Pharaoh is still stubborn against the request of Moses to free the people. The ultimate challenge, which was a challenge to Pharaoh's person, his kingship, and his divinity, was a showdown about life and death, over which the pharaohs were believed to have ultimate control. The way to break the king, since the contest between every other divine notion of Egypt didn't bring about the freedom of his people, was on the pivotal and supreme issue of life and death.

In addition, we need to understand that all Egypt was complicit—guilty—of infanticide of the Israelites. The king had given an order to the whole population to kill Israelite children (Exodus 1.22). In

---

[82] In the Bible there are hints that babies who die go to heaven because they were incapable of rational, moral decisions, and God doesn't hold people accountable for decisions when they are completely incapable of decisions. (1) Dt. 1.37-40: God's people are being judged for their rebellion, but the young ones who didn't have the mental capacity to make a reasoned and moral decision like that don't get judged. (2) Number 14.29 speaks of a kind of "age of accountability," just as Dt. 1.37-40 did. (3) Isa. 7.15. People can be too young mentally to know enough to reject the wrong and choose the right.

Exodus 1.9-14, all Egypt treated the Israelites cruelly, and oppressed them harshly (look at Exodus 4.22, where God says that Israel is his firstborn son). God's judgment on the children of Egypt was simply an eye for an eye—let the punishment fit the crime, no more, no less.

While a superficial impression might be that it was Pharaoh who sinned and not the Egyptian people, the people were not innocent bystanders. The Egyptians were part of the enslavement of the Israelites. Don't they share responsibility for the persecution of them? We indict the German people, and even the German church, for standing passive while Hitler exterminated Jews in WWII. Isn't failure to do what is right a sin?

Regardless of how you evaluate the use of nuclear weapons at the end of WWII, dropping atomic bombs on Hiroshima and Nagasaki was designed to send a message to the Japanese government that assassination of their emperor and prime minister would not have accomplished. The judgments of YHWH (again, characteristic of all 10 plagues) had to affect the whole nation or they wouldn't mean anything. The only way to speak to the deception and fallacies of their mythologies and the national nature of their murderous sin was to act in a way that included the entire nation. Because the king and the nation had demonstrated their cruelty, we understand the fairness of the sentence.

It might also help to understand that in the ancient Near East they viewed corporate (national) entities as indivisible unities. They were a community of people together, sharing the blessings of one as the blessings of all, and the cursing of one as the cursing of all. Their perception is that they rose and fell together as a clan or community. Despite the fact that a one-year-old in our mindset is an innocent baby, in *their* mindset a one-year-old was part of the community, subject to divine blessings and divine judgment as much as anyone else. In their mindset, a strike at the children was not a strike against innocents (as it seems to us in our modern mentality), but a strike against the core perceptions of the community (the firstborn were the family priests) and the depravity of their religious system (Pharaoh as the giver of life to babies).

Lastly, I have already explained in the previous section that there was no command of God to slaughter babies in the Conquest.

Joshua and the people would not have understood the rhetoric to mean infanticide, nor interpreted God's command that way. No Israelite was hacking or stabbing babies or children.

ACCUSATION: GOD IS EVIL
BECAUSE HE IS GUILTY OF **MISOGYNY**
(THE REPRESSION OF WOMEN).

The accusation of misogyny in the Bible reflects a misunderstanding of the biblical text. In Genesis 1.26, we can see in that verse that both the male and female were the image of God, positioned as equals in essence. Both are mandated in Gn. 1.28 to rule the earth and subdue it as equal co-regents of God. In Gn. 2, one of the points of the text is that male and female are ontologically unified as equals. Her identity is that she is his ally, his partner, his equal, his other half.[83] "Helper" is not a marker of inferiority; most of the time in the Old Testament when the term is used it is used of God and his relation to Israel. An honest study of the text shows that both the "help meet" concept and the "rib" event are specifically (linguistically and contextually) showing how woman is every much his equal—equal in status and in worth, equal in role and function, and equal in godlikeness.

The Mosaic Law regularly includes and commands provisions so that the rights of women are not ignored, and so that she is treated as a person of value.

The narrative accounts in the Old Testament tell the stories of many noble and heroic women, including Jocabed, Miriam, Deborah, Ruth, Abigail, and Esther.

In the Gospels we read repeatedly how Jesus treated women with dignity, and how he refused to play into the misogyny of his culture. He had many women followers. Women were at his birth, his dedication, the cross, and the tomb.

Paul, in Ephesians 5.21-33, shows how the gospel lifts women from cultural degradation to a place of honor. 1 Corinthians 11 shows how women could pray and prophecy in their gatherings just as the

---

[83] John Walton, The Lost World of Adam and Eve (Downers Grove, IL: InterVarsity Press, 2015), p. 80

men did. Carol Meyers[84] contributes to the discussion with this cultural analysis of ancient Israel (excerpts):

> While there were certain activities in the household that the women exclusively did, such as the grinding of grain into flour, anthropologists note that most household activities were not performed exclusively by one gender. ...
>
> Anthropological studies can also elucidate women's relationships with other members of their families, especially their husbands. Were women really as subordinate in Biblical times as many people think? Anthropological studies from societies similar to ancient Israel provide useful analogies. Interactions between household members are an example. Because women often have critical roles in maintaining household life, the senior woman in an extended family is often in a position of parity and interdependence, not subordination, with her husband for most aspects of household life. This is an especially significant observation for ancient Israel because the household was the major unity of society for most Israelites. ...
>
> The negative images of Eve that persist until today can be traced to ancient sources beginning in the Greco-Roman world. Those images were influenced by ideas about women that were current in Greco-Roman times but not in Iron Age Israel. ...
>
> Social scientists alert us to what they call "presentism," the phenomenon in which perspectives and ideas that we take for granted in today's world affect how we understand the past. We tend to read the present into the past anachronistically, which can lead us to misunderstanding the past. It is surely true that human beings have much in common throughout time, but there are also sometimes basic differences, and these must be taken into account. For example, today

---

[84] " 'Eves' of Everyday Ancient Israel" by Carol L. Meyers, *Biblical Archaeology Review,* November/December 2014, pp. 51-54, 66, 68

cooking and cleaning and caring for young children are often seen as unpaid housework. These chores may be undervalued, even trivialized. But in a pre-modern peasant society without supermarkets and day-care centers, these tasks have significant economic value. They are essential for household survival, and they earn women positive regard.

Similarly, "presentism" can affect how we view the division between work and family, between what is public and what is private. How these divisions are understood may be very different between a post-industrial capitalist society, on the one hand, and a pre-modern agrarian society on the other. In the latter, the household is the workplace for both women and men, and household activities for both women and men were connected to larger community and kinship structures.

Consider the concept of patriarchy. Typically this concept has been taken to imply near total male domination in families and in other social institutions. But anthropologists, classicists, feminist theorists, theologians and others who have more recently studied the concept have shown that this understanding of patriarchy does not take into account that women often had considerable agency in certain aspects of household life and that women's groups and institutions had their own hierarchies. ...

To get a balanced view of Israelite society in the Iron Age, the broader picture must be considered. Patriarchy is a term that was invented millennia after the Iron Age and is probably unsuitable for characterizing ancient Israel.

A common Bible text often mistakenly used to justify misogyny is 1 Timothy 2.11-15. There Paul says a woman is not allowed to speak, must remain silent and fully submissive. She is not permitted to teach or exercise authority over men. We can know, first of all, that Paul's words have a particular local meaning (to this particular church, as opposed to a universal principle) since in 1 Corinthians 11 (esp. v. 5) he teaches that women are allowed to speak (pray and prophecy) in the assembly as long as their head was covered – another local teaching. We also know that one of the general themes of 1 Timothy is the campaign against false teachers. Like Eve, the women of the situation addressed in 1 Timothy were likely listening to and propagating false teaching and asserting their position over wiser, orthodox authority. This was not to be. (Remember, in their culture the women were not educated routinely as men were.) All false teachers, in this case, women, needed to remain silent and submit to the authority of true teaching. People not versed in the truth need to learn submissively rather than assert themselves against those who *are* teaching the truth. The passage (along with Paul, the Bible, and God Himself) is not misogynistic, but concerned that the truth be paramount.

ACCUSATION: GOD IS EVIL BECAUSE HE CREATED HELL AND PUTS PEOPLE THERE.

The objections to hell are so numerous they are a cacophony of voices echoing from every corner. Even Christians voice concern over not only the perceived unfairness of hell, but even its very existence. Here are some quotes from skeptics and critics:

- Hell is one of my biggest sticking points.
- Why would a good God send a good person to hell?
- What purpose does hell serve?
- Why don't I get a chance to choose *after* I die?
- Hell is a defeater for a loving God.
- Does anyone really deserve an eternity of torture? Do most of us?

Not all Christians, you should know, believe in the traditional concept of hell. There are theories about reconcilationism, semi-restorationism, modified eternalism, and annihilationism, all with some kind of scriptural backing. Scripturally, the subject of hell is impossible to avoid. Let's talk about it.

First let me make it crystal clear that hell was not created for people, and it was never God's intent that people would go there. Hell was created for Satan and his angels (Matthew 25.41), period! Hell was not made for people; heaven was made for people. This is not to imply that God was somehow surprised by sin. His plan of redemption through Christ was set in place before the creation of the world.

Let's look at the issue logically and legally, rather than emotionally. Any judge who is worth his salt vindicates good people and punishes bad people. That's what the courts and justice are all about: the bad guys aren't supposed to get away with it—they're supposed to get caught and face the consequences.

There are different kinds of justice. Distributive justice basically deals with the decision of who gets it, and retributive justice deals with the decision of how much—the severity, leniency, or appropriateness of the sentence..

For instance, in a company, if everyone gets the same pay raise no matter how hard they worked, what their level of success, how many sales they made, etc., this would be perceived as distributively unjust. Rewards and punishments should be allocated fairly to the appropriate people.

Retributive justice deals with the question of how much. It's the philosophy where "the punishment should fit the crime." Greater infractions should yield more dire consequences.

Hell, then, is certainly portrayed as an exercise of justice. A wrong has been perpetrated, and for justice to be served, balance must be reinstated in a system now askew. If punishment and reward are issued to the correct people in appropriate amounts, we would consider the situation to be fair, and restored to equilibrium.

The first tier of justice is that the sentence should most appropriately be pronounced by someone with both the authority and the integrity to issue the verdict and pronounce the consequences. This person would be the Holy and righteous God.

The second tier of justice: The rewards and punishments are delivered on the basis of personal decisions that cogent people intentionally made. Those who want to spend eternity with God get their desire, and those who don't also get their desire.

What about those who never heard, or those too young or mentally incapacitated to decide? That will all be taken into account.

- Romans 5.13: People won't be held accountable for what they didn't know or could not have known.
- Deuteronomy 1.37-40; Numbers 14.29; Isaiah 7.15: People won't be held accountable for decisions they were mentally incapable of making.

The third tier of justice: The rewards and punishments will fit the infraction. Hell is not a "One Fire Tortures All." (I don't even think hell is fire. That's just a metaphor to describe the awfulness of separation from God.) We have strong hints that there are different degrees of punishment in hell (totally unlike the different levels of hell as in Dante's *Divine Comedy*, which is not Scripture).

- Matthew 11.22-24 & Luke 10.12: Jesus says it will be "more tolerable" for the people of Sodom and Gomorrah than for the people of Capernaum. That would indicate to me a more harsh punishment and a less harsh punishment.
- Matthew 23.14: Jesus tells the Pharisees they will be punished more severely for the way they are deceiving the people and living as hypocrites.
- Revelation 20.13: Each is going to be judged according to what he has done. Since that is the case, then the punishments and rewards can't be the same for everybody.
- and finally, Luke 12.47-48 (workers are punished with more or fewer blows). There are degrees of punishment, and even sins of ignorance are treated differently than sins of intention.

Why I bother to point this out is because often those who consider hell to be unfair are picturing the same punishment for all, which is most likely not the case, and infinite punishment for finite crimes, which may also not be the case. People will be punished according to the works they have done (2 Corinthians 5.10).

There seem to be only two possible scenarios: (1) God somehow takes a perverse pleasure about sending people to hell with a callous disregard and disengagement from any emotional bondage to the reality of what is happening, or (2) God somehow is filled with love and is crying as people are cast forth from his presence. Well, anyone who reads anything about the God of the Bible knows that the first choice is impossible, so somehow we must make sense of the second.

- God has both perfect love and perfect justice. We misunderstand if we think the two are competing values where one has to win out over the other. Any parent knows that love also involved punishment for wrong choices. To be truthful we must show how love and justice can both be present together to an infinite and noncontradictory extent.
- The picture of people screaming in agony, floating around alone in a lake of fire has to be dismissed. The biblical teaching of degrees of punishment cannot allow for this unrealistic portrayal. Despite many traditional evangelical beliefs, it shows a shallow and inaccurate reading of the "hell" texts. Don't be mistaken, though: the metaphor of fire and brimstone is to point to an unspeakable horror—that of being truly separated from the presence of God.
- We have to grasp that people go to hell by their own choice, not by God's, that no one in hell has been sent there apart from their will, and that they will agree with God's casting them there, for it's the desire of their hearts, as weird as that may sound. After all, the sin of Adam and Eve, and the root of sin in all of us, is self: pride, independence, and personal power. Each of us knows someone who chooses a self-destructive path in life despite all pleadings to the contrary. It's much the same as people who choose God or self. If it's self, then it's self.

Allow me to explain each point in sufficient detail to lead you to understanding.

1. Love is an act of the will, not an emotion. It must be chosen, not forced, or it's not love. We choose to act in the interest of someone else. God loves us, and both will not and cannot interfere with our free will. If I can only love God because I'm caused to do it and I have no choice, that's not love at all. If God interferes with my free will to constrain me to love him, that is nothing more than a contradiction, and negating what love is. All of us have a choice in life: to align with God and become one with Him, or to choose not to align with God and be separated from Him. Like pregnancy, there's no halfway. You either are or you aren't. So to be consistent in His nature and not self-contradictory, He has to allow those who wish to be aligned with Him to come, and He has to allow those who wish to be separate from Him to do so. As it turns out, these are the definitions of heaven and hell. Everything with God is based in relationship— even eternity. So His great act of love is to allow us the freedom to choose (see also Romans 1.22-23). As it turns out, it is also perfectly just, for in eternity the Bible is clear that God's judgment over us is not based on our works, but our relationship. Those who choose to have the nature of Jesus (not just those who are good) go to heaven, and those who choose not to have the nature of Jesus (not just those who are "bad") are allowed to remain separate from Him. His justice aligns perfectly with His love in that everyone has the relationship with Him that they choose and spend eternity, in all fairness, in what they chose.

2. Hell is not, as I said, people floating in a sea of raging fire, screaming at the top of their lungs in sheer agony for eternity. I know I part ways with traditional evangelicalism at this point, but for a reason. As I've said, the Bible teaches degrees of punishment in hell: the FIRE part is what Satan and his angels will experience (Matthew 25.41). What is "hell" for people, then? It is death, or separation from Life, which is God (2 Thessalonians 1.7-9; Revelation 20.14); it is suffering and remorse (indubitably), it is punishment (Matthew 25.46; Rev. 14.11), and it is God's judgment,

symbolized by fire in some texts, by being cut to pieces in some, and by darkness in others. What does this "separation from God" (Matthew 7.23; 25.41; Daniel 12.3; Romans 2.5) mean? The only choice is a counterpart of what heaven is. It is the agony of unmitigated absence from God, emptiness, day in and day out meaninglessness, argumentation, insecurity, the pain of everything being wrong, dissatisfaction, and fear. That's right: life as we know it now, but without any of the redeeming blessings of life that come from God. Heaven isn't jewels and harps; hell isn't screaming and fire. Heaven is daily glory (the essence of God's being), and hell is daily death (the essence of sin). Jesus' verbal images are his chosen expression to let everyone know hell is the worst of all possible worlds and is to be avoided at all costs.

3. They don't WANT a relationship with God. They choose self instead of God. The only reason they would want to go to heaven is to avoid suffering, which is understandable. Here's the truth: there are two choices: Be connected with God thoroughly and relationally, or not be connected. For those who choose not to be connected, God sends them from his presence. It's an act of love, because love won't override the other person's will to get what he wants. As you read *all* the stories of Jesus, you will observe that the people who get sent to hell in the parables are the people who chose self over God. Hell is choice and self-preservation on the part of the people making the decision (see also Romans 1.22-23). God, in love and with a broken heart, lets them go away from him, even sends them. We see it many times in the Gospels: Jesus will not stay where he is not wanted.

C.S. Lewis makes some interesting observations about hell. I'll reword them and summarize some of them here: You object to the doctrine of hell. What are you asking God to do? To wipe out past sins at all costs and to give anyone who wants it a fresh start, smoothing difficulties and offering help? But He has DONE that. That's what his death and resurrection were all about. OK, then, are you asking God to forgive you? It's a RELATIONSHIP. He will forgive anyone who wants it, and cannot forgive those who choose not to be forgiven. To leave you alone then? Well, I'm afraid that's what hell is.

If a game is played, it must be possible to lose it. If there is a way that must be found by the will, and by love, then it must be possible to refuse it. If the happiness of a person is honestly the result of self-surrender, then no one can make that decision except himself, and he may refuse. I would love to say everyone will be saved. But then I'd have to ask, "Will they be saved against their will, or with it?" If I say "against their will," I'm in the middle of a contradiction; how can self-surrender and love be involuntary? But if the answer is "With their will," it begs the question: "What if they will not give in?"

The Bible speaks of two possible natures a person can have: a sin nature (born with it), where a person is separated from the life of God, or the nature of Jesus, where a person shares the life of God (requires a second birth). The Bible talks about it metaphorically as light and darkness, life and death, even sheep and goats.

Hell (and heaven for that matter) have nothing to do with good and bad. Those who love God and wish to share his life and spend eternity with him can. The invitation is open to anyone. Those who don't love God, and don't wish to share his life or spend eternity with him aren't forced to. They can have what they will, and can be separated from God.

Does the existence of hell mean that God is not loving? Far from it. Hell is not where God throws people he doesn't love anymore. Hell is where people choose to go who don't want anything to do with a relationship with God. I can say with confidence that God doesn't want anyone to go to hell. You misunderstand if you think that God somehow stops loving people and sends them to hell when they no longer please him. God opens the doors of heaven and invites everyone in, but many people simply refuse to come, despite his promises of blessing, his intent to reward, his desire for relationship, and his personal sacrifice to make it free for anyone to come. Hell (separation from God) is the only other choice for people who don't wish to be united with God. It doesn't make God evil to allow you to make your own choice, and not to force you to love him (which isn't love at all). When all is said and done, you know about God, you know about the message of the Bible saying that he is love, that he is fair, and that he wants a relationship with you, you know the warnings about rebellion against him, and you know the consequences of your own decisions and actions. You make your choice, and you live with the results.

So, with all that has been said, and with all the disagreements, even from Christians, about hell, I can conclude with confidence with this statement: **Those who turn away from God will be separated from the life of God. Though we can't be sure about the form or duration of that separation, this we can be sure of: it will be a horrible experience, and God will be fair about the form and duration of it. If you reject God, you take your chances.**

ACCUSATION: MIRACLES ARE NOT POSSIBLE

The first step in any discussion about miracles is to define a miracle. Some philosophers say that it is an occurrence contrary to nature,[85] but we shouldn't be so quick to embrace that definition and then find our hands tied by our own definition. The Bible never claims that God violated the laws he himself imposed on the world. Maybe a miracle is God working with the laws of nature rather than against them, just in a different manner and on a different time scale. C.S. Lewis, for one, said that miracles were just nature on a different time continuum, like *fast forward*. He said water always turns to wine; it just usually takes four months instead of one second; human bodies have the capability to heal, just not instantaneously at the word of the Master. So what is a miracle?

I would tentatively define miracle as "a supernatural exception to the regularity and predictability of the universe, and therefore it is not a common (this term needs to be interpreted) occurrence." Maybe the laws of nature speak of naturally recurring events, and miracles speak of supernaturally nonrecurring events. After all, the laws of nature are not really laws, but rather more accurately forces (gravitational, electromagnetic, weak and strong field forces) and

---

[85] David Hume defines a miracle as "a suspension of nature".

constructs (velocity, mass, energy, acceleration).[86] Einstein's theory of relativity lets us know that velocity makes a difference in reality and can come into play in ways we are still deciphering. It's quite possible that God has forces as yet unknown to us, and can manipulate velocity, as well as other forces, to initiate relative states.

Secondly, we should realize that science cannot prove that miracles are impossible. After all, science can only speak to what is within the purview of scientific observation and the study of nature. Anything outside of that ballpark is outside of its scope. Science can't prove to us whether entities exist outside of nature, and whether or not those entities could possibly have an influence in our natural world. Here's a lengthy excerpt from a conversation C.S. Lewis had with a friend:[87]

> 'Miracles,' said my friend. 'Oh, come. Science has knocked the bottom out of all that. We know that Nature is governed by fixed laws.'

> 'Didn't people always know that?' said I.

> 'Good Lord, no,' said he. 'For instance, take a story like the Virgin Birth. We know now that such a thing couldn't happen. We know there must be a male spermatozoon.'

> 'But look here,' said I, 'St. Joseph—,'

> 'Who's he?' asked my friend.

> 'He was the husband of the Virgin Mary. If you'll read the story in the Bible you'll find that when he saw his fiancée was going to have a baby he decided to cry off the marriage. Why did he do that?'

[86] Charles E. Hummel, The Galileo Connection (Downers Grove, IL: InterVarsity Press, 1986), pp. 194-195

[87] C.S. Lewis, God in the Dock (Grand Rapids, MI: William B. Eerdmans Publishing Co., 1970) pp. 72-74

'Wouldn't most men?'

'Any man would,' said I, 'provided he knew the laws of Nature—in other words, provided he knew that a girl doesn't ordinarily have a baby unless she's been sleeping with a man. But according to your theory people in the old days didn't know that Nature was governed by fixed laws. I'm pointing out that the story shows that St. Joseph knew that law just as well as you do.'

'But he came to believe in the Virgin Birth afterwards, didn't he?'

'Quite. But he didn't do so because he was under any illusion as to where babies came from in the ordinary course of Nature. He believed in the Virgin Birth as something supernatural. He knew Nature works in fixed, regular ways: but he also believed that there existed something beyond Nature which could interfere with her workings—from outside, so to speak.'

'But modern science has shown there's no such thing.'

'Really,' said I. 'Which of the sciences?'

'Oh, well, that's a matter of detail,' said my friend. 'I can't give you chapter and verse from memory.'

'But, don't you see,' said I, 'that science never could show anything of the sort?'

'Why on earth not?'

'Because science studies Nature. And the question is whether anything besides Nature exists— anything "outside". How could you find that out by studying simply Nature?'

'But don't we find out that Nature must work in an absolutely fixed way? I mean, the laws of Nature tell us not merely how things do happen, but how they must happen. No power could possibly alter them.'

'How do you mean?' said I.

'Look here,' said he. 'Could this "something outside" that you talk about make two and two five?'

'Well, no.' said I.

'All right.' said he. 'Well, I think the laws of Nature are really like two and two making four. The idea of their being altered is as absurd as the idea of altering the laws of arithmetic.'

'Half a moment.' said I. 'Suppose you put sixpence into a drawer today, and sixpence into the same drawer tomorrow. Do the laws of arithmetic make it certain you'll find a shilling's worth there the day after?'

'Of course,' said he, 'provided no one's been tampering with your drawer.'

'Ah, but that's the whole point,' said I. 'The laws of arithmetic can tell you what you'll find, with absolute certainty, provided that there's no interference. If a thief has been at the drawer of course you'll get a different result. But the thief won't have broken the laws of arithmetic—only the laws of England. Now, aren't the laws of Nature much in the same boat? Don't they all tell you what will happen provided there's no interference?'

'How do you mean?'

'Well, the laws will tell you how a billiard ball will travel on a smooth surface if you hit it in a particular way—but only provided no one interferes. If, after it's already in motion, someone snatches up a cue and gives it a biff on one side—why, then, you won't get what the scientist predicted.'

'No, of course not. He can't allow for monkey-tricks like that.'

'Quite, and in the same way, if there was anything outside Nature, and if it interfered—then the events which the scientist expected wouldn't follow. That would be what we call a miracle. In one sense it wouldn't break the laws of Nature. The laws tell you what will happen if nothing interferes. They can't tell you whether something is going to interfere. I mean, it's not the expert at arithmetic who can tell you how likely someone is to interfere with the pennies in my drawer; a detective would be more use. It isn't the physicist who can tell you how likely I am to catch up a cue and spoil his experiment with the billiard ball; you'd better ask a psychologist. And it isn't the scientist who can tell you how likely Nature is to be interfered with from outside. You must go to the metaphysician.'

Since a miracle, by *any* definition, is a once only, nonrecurring event, it is outside the scope of science (which can only observe and test recurring sequences) and naturalistic evidence. Miracles can only be proven in two ways: (1) that they can be shown to be logically consistent with the physical world—the way things are, or (2) by enough corroborating, credible eyewitnesses to substantiate the claim being made.

Reviewing Lewis's story, if I put $20 in your pocket today, and then another $20 in there tomorrow, logic and reason would tell me that there will be $40 in your pocket. And of course that's true, provided that no one has meddled in your pocket. So one of the first things to establish when we discuss the possibility of miracles is to find out whether your presuppositions have ruled out all "meddling" by definition. In that case, of course miracles are impossible to prove. You have made it impossible by your arbitrary definition. The second thing to notice is that nature is full of once-only, non-recurring events, such as the cosmic blast that happened in Russia in 2013. It would be sort of foolish for a group of scientists to gather there saying, "C'mon, do it again!"

As far as the second, if you have enough trustworthy people whose eyewitness accounts corroborate with each other, even though the event may not repeat, it could be considered to be accepted as reality. Even our courts rely on such testimony as acceptable.

There is no philosophical argument or scientific experiment that conclusively disproves the possibility of miracles. Scientifically speaking, the odds of certain miracles occurring (such as the resurrection) may be infinity to one, but theologically speaking they are x:x (unknown to unknown). Miracles are outside of the scope of probability calculations. But realistically, the question is not so much "Can they occur?" but "Do they occur?" Anyone will admit that scientists exclude the miraculous from their scientific work, which they are entitled to do. But that's because if a scientist tried to offer a miraculous explanation for something, he or she would no longer be doing science, but something else, like theology or philosophy. Miracles are inadmissible as scientific evidence because they are unpredictable, not able to be compared with a control group, and unrepeatable for confirmatory studies.

Ultimately you are asking the wrong question of the wrong discipline. Science can really only work in a uniform environment that is predictable, repeatable, and (in this situation) controllable (a control group and an experimental group). Evidentiary demands require some sort of material remains that allow a phenomenon to be studied, but this requirement is outside of the sphere of what we mean by "miracle." Miracles are not predictable (so the situation can't be intentionally studied before the event), reproducible (so the situation can't be tested again to confirm hypotheses), nor controllable (cannot isolate causal mechanisms).

Science is appropriate when dealing with repeatable (reproducible) phenomena that can be studied under controlled conditions and give confirmatory results. One time events that were not predictable and don't leave behind any material evidence can't possibly fall under that category. Suppose you had a sneezing fit a few weeks back. I want you to quantify it and analyze it, or better yet, prove to me that it happened. That's not possible, Should I then assume you never sneeze, never sneezed, and that you're wrong until you can prove it? What evidence do you have that you had a sneezing fit? Or walked around the mall last month? Or saw a catamount? We have to use the proper measure for the proper category. And science is not the proper measure for understanding or proving miracles. Even in the area of astronomy, for instance, where some phenomena are one-time only events, to study them scientifically requires multiple repeatable examples that can be observed and compared/contrasted. Again, miracles don't fall into this category.

In short, the bottom line is that knowledge is not one-dimensional. The methods of evidentiary scientific study are not applicable to much of our knowledge, including the occasion of miracles. Attempting to extend scientific evidence as the grounds of all knowledge is doomed to failure in many arenas, not just this one. To presume that anything remaining outside of science's scope fails to qualify as knowledge is not justified by science or any other argument, and is, in fact, self-contradictory.

Can anyone prove that a once-only nonrecurring event is a miracle from God or not? No, because either way it's an interpretation of what one has seen or experienced. We all decide based on what we determine to be consistent with our understanding of the world and the evidences on which we build those understandings.

Let's talk a little bit about Newtonian physics and miracles. People's main problem with miracles is that they mess with what people know about science, while at the same time requiring them (if accepted) to subscribe to metaphysical realities like spirits and spiritual forces. But if we are honest philosophers and scientists, we have to be open to reputable questions (as any scientist would ask): Why can't the causal continuum be interfered with by supernatural and transcendent powers? Why are miracles necessarily incompatible with modern science? A little probing will reveal that they are not. They are only incompatible if it can be proved that nature is a closed continuum of cause and effect, and closed to any intervention from outside that continuum. Classical (Newtonian) science is nowhere near sufficient for anti-interventionism. Newton himself believed that the laws he observed reflected the nature of what God had created. According to Newton, natural law describes how the world works when, or provided that, the world is a closed system, subject to no meddling. The Newtonian laws of physics only apply to isolated or closed systems, but there is nothing in them to say there is or can be no God who can intervene in such a system to make change to the matter or energy in question. Furthermore, it is not part of Newtonian mechanics or classical science generally to declare that the material universe *is* a closed system— because that claim isn't scientific, but theological, philosophical, or metaphysical. The laws don't tell us how things *have* to go, or even how they *always* go, but only how they go when no outside agency acts on them.

Interestingly, quantum mechanics offers even less of a problem for special divine action than classical science, since quantum mechanics is characterized by (among other things) indeterminism: a spectrum of probabilities to the possible outcomes. Quantum mechanics doesn't by necessity prohibit any answers to prayer, raising the dead, or walking on the water.

Looking at miracles even another way, it's absurd to think that everything must be subject to scientific proof and evidence, and miracles are in that category as well. We are wrong even to think that miracles should be or can be subject to scientific inquiry. There are thousands of things we know that are not subject to scientific proof (as critics want miracles to be): I like apple pie, I forgive you, I felt chilly yesterday, I saw a beautiful sunset five days ago, Bill is my friend, that wasn't fair, I'm in love with Denise, I'm afraid of heights, my favorite movie is "Gladiator," I feel at peace with myself. There are millions of these. We're just in the wrong arena to think that we can use science to prove these things. There are also things that exist, that are coherent, but not scientific: peace, justice, love, memory, reason, values, to name a few. There are disciplines that have nothing to do with science, but they are still legitimate ways to know things: jurisprudence, economics, history, literature, politics, art, philosophy, logic, and theology. As it turns out, probably most of what we know is not subject to scientific verification, nor can it be considered scientific knowledge. Miracles also fall into this category. It is both illogical and unreasonable to apply scientific reason or necessity to the possibility or veracity of miracles. While we can bring some scientific thinking to bear as we evaluate them, they are just as much outside of the purview of science as "I forgive you."

ACCUSATION: CREATION BY GOD (THE GENESIS ACCOUNT) AND EVOLUTION ARE INCOMPATIBLE, AND SINCE WE KNOW EVOLUTION IS TRUE, CREATION BY GOD IS PROVED FALSE.

Our first step in unraveling this misunderstanding is to establish that "evolution" can mean different things:

1. The process of change
2. The development of species to their present state, through minor and major change
3. Evolutionism (a.k.a. scientific naturalism): a faith philosophy based on thoughts that nature and matter are all that exists, and all that exists is the result of impersonal forces plus time plus chance.

The first two are not a problem for the Christian, but the third definitely is. So it matters what you're talking about when you use the word "evolution." Here is why the first two are not a problem:

1. Science is spiritually and morally neutral. We wouldn't say chemistry is godless, or that physics is godly. Science is science, godliness is godliness. Let's not tether the two together.

2. There is an unnecessary linkage between evolution and godlessness. Instead, it's more accurate to say that evolutionary theory is a worldview that is spiritually neutral, dependent on good science for verification or invalidation, independent of any religious or atheistic connection. Evolution doesn't undermine our faith unless we define it as "a godless process," which is not the necessary definition.

3. The Bible clearly tells us *that* God created, but not specifically how it happened, how long it took, or what processes, if any, were used. Even in the traditional approach, we don't know how it happened except that God spoke. But did it pop, did it grow, was there a flash, did it fade in? We still don't know how it happened. As Galileo said, "The Bible tells us how to go to heaven, not how the heavens go."

4. Process is not contrary to the idea of God being the creator, and evolution as a process can have validity if we perceive God's power and design flowing through the process. God is involved in this world in many hidden ways—read the book of Esther, or even the first four chapters of 2 Samuel about David's ascent to the throne. We know that sometimes it's hard to discern God's hand, but we know it's there. We just don't always know how it's all working.

5. The ancients saw no distinction between natural and supernatural processes, so the concept of process is not foreign to biblical "miracles." Nor is process foreign to "God did it." In the following Biblical texts, there is no distinct line between the natural and the supernatural.
   - The flood: Gn. 6-8. Rain came from the sky, the earth opened up and waters rose from underground reservoirs. Was it all special activity, or did God use some natural processes?
   - The parting of the Reed Sea: Exodus 14.21: "all night long the Lord drove the sea back with a strong

wind." God used a natural process to accomplish his work.

- The provision of quail: Ex. 16.13. Quail occasionally did blow in with the winds. God uses natural processes.

6. Evolution doesn't rule out our doctrine of original sin. Original sin is an inviolable Christian doctrine, regardless of the science. At some point in time, not necessarily known to us, humanity became spiritually culpable, failed the test, and sin came upon all humanity. There is no reason to consider that a process of creation negates that doctrine, and it certainly doesn't necessarily do it.

Evolutionary processes are not the problem, but only scientific naturalism, which says there is no God and there were no outside forces at work in the evolutionary process. But there is nothing in either the Genesis account or evolution that makes them inherently contradictory ideas.

ACCUSATION: JESUS DIDN'T FULFILL MESSIANIC PROPHECY

As people talk to me about Jesus, they express their strong opinions that Jesus was not the promised Messiah because he didn't fulfill the Messianic prophecies.

"The Bible is not all about Jesus. None of it is about Jesus, and most of it isn't about the messiah. I could twist the whole thing into being a prophecy about Spongebob if I tried hard enough."

"Even if Jesus had came back from the dead it still wouldn't make him the messiah, since he failed to fulfill any of the messianic prophecies."

When people want to talk about messianic prophecies, they generally want to talk about specific texts, the "fingerprints" of messianic prophecies scattered about the Old Testament, where God marked out, "This is a prophecy about the Messiah." Some are debatable, but some are widely agreed upon. A brief survey of such prophecies reads:

- Genesis 49.10, speaking of a king from the tribe of Judah who will rule the nations.
- 2 Samuel 7.13, speaking of a king from the house of David who will establish a throne
- Psalm 2, speaking of a king who will be installed in Jerusalem to rule the nations
- Psalm 110, speaking of a king who will rule from Jerusalem and subdue his enemies
- Isaiah 4, speaking of a day when Jerusalem will be restored to glory
- Isaiah 9.6, speaking of a wonderful king
- Isaiah 11-12, speaking of a king who will judge wisely, rule with righteousness, and subdue his enemies
- Isaiah 14, speaking of a king who will subdue his enemies
- Isaiah 53, speaking of a suffering servant
- Isaiah 55, speaking of a splendor-adorned king
- Jeremiah 3.17, speaking of a king in Jerusalem
- Jeremiah 23.5, speaking of righteous king who will rule wisely
- Jeremiah 30.9, speaking of a king
- Jeremiah 33.15, speaking of a king who will rule with justice
- Micah 1, speaking of a king who will establish justice, peace, security, and compassion
- Micah 5.2, speaking of the messianic king who will be born in Bethlehem
- Zechariah 14, speaking of the nature of the messianic kingdom

One can readily see that these texts speak of a righteous political ruler, with a throne in Jerusalem, subduing the nations and ruling with justice and power. But what of Jesus, then, who never established an earthly kingdom?

The problem arises when one is looking for Jesus only in certain Old Testament texts instead of throughout its entirety. A more accurate perspective of Jesus is to recognize that he said all of the Old Testament was prophetic about him (Matthew 5.17; Luke 24.27), not just the specifically messianic texts. A brief survey of the Scriptures reads:

- Genesis 1: John 1 and Hebrews 1 tell us that Jesus was the creator, that he is light and life (John 1.4), and that all things were made by him. In Jesus' resurrection he will bring light and life where there was only darkness and death.
- Genesis 2: Jesus is Lord of the Sabbath (Matthew 12.8) and the new Adam (Romans 5). He is the source of all life and wisdom.
- Genesis 3: Jesus came to undo the problem of sin in the human heart. He is the seed of the woman who will crush the head of the serpent.
- Genesis 4 is about acceptable offerings to God. While Genesis 4 is not about Jesus per se, it is true that Jesus is the acceptable offering to God, the blood of the sacrifice.
- Genesis 5: Enoch shows us reality of an afterlife that comes as a result of Jesus' resurrection. Jesus is the one who will truly comfort us in the labor and painful toil of our hands (Gn. 5.29; Mt. 11.28-30).
- Genesis 6-8: Jesus is the judge of the earth (Jn. 5.22; 2 Cor. 5.10). The flood is a type of baptism as death and resurrection (1 Pet. 3.20-21).
- Genesis 9: Jesus' resurrection is the real sign of the everlasting covenant of life.
- Genesis 10 foreshadows the rule of Jesus over every tribe, language, people and nation (Phil. 2.11; Rev. 7.9).
- Genesis 11 is reversed in Acts 2 when Jesus comes in the Spirit to fill his people.
- Genesis 12: It is through Jesus that all nations on earth will ultimately be blessed.

We could continue this through the entire biblical text. All of the Old Testament Scriptures, not just the "fingerprints," speak of Jesus, his coming, his character, his work, and his reign.

ACCUSATION: THE DEATH OF ONE MAN CANNOT FORGIVE THE SINS OF ALL

Some things in life can be handled with a substitute, and some can't. If I have a debt and someone steps forward to pay the debt for me, I will be grateful for his or her gift, and the matter is resolved. Other situations can't be handled by substitution. If a man murders my wife, and someone else steps forward to serve his prison time for him so the perpetrator can go free, that doesn't seem fair to me. The Bible says that Jesus' death for us has elements of both in it. He is paying the debt for us, and that's a legitimate solution to the debt of sin. And while the latter may not logically seem fair, legally it works.

The Law of God required death for sin. That's justice. But from the beginning God said that he would accept the blood sacrifice of a substitute as payment. At the same time he gave the Law he also gave the sacrificial system. It was always a system of penal substitutionary atonement: The "crime" of sin could be satisfied with an appropriate substitution. While we may scratch our heads at the pure logic of the thing, God has said that he would accept the life of an innocent substitute (a lamb) in exchange for the life of the guilty party (a human). That way God can enforce justice (death has to be the end result in accordance with justice) but also exercise mercy (it doesn't have to be *you* that dies).

Sin in the Bible is not a singular simple entity. The Bible variously defines it as ignorance, inattention, error, missing the mark, irreligion, transgression, rebellion, treachery, unbelief, perversion, evil, guilt, etc. Some of the concepts focus on its causes, others on its nature, and still others on its consequences. It's not just a simple notion.

And, as David Brooks says, "There are not only different kinds of sin, but different remedies for each. Some sins, like anger and lust, are like wild beasts. They have to be fought through habits of restraint. Some sins, like mockery and disrespect, are like stains. They can only be expunged by apology, remorse, restitution, and cleansing. Some sins, like stealing, are like a debt. They can only be rectified by repaying what you owe to society. Some sins, like adultery, bribery, and betrayal, are more like treason than crime; they are affronts to the social order. The social harmony can only be rewoven by slowly recommitting to relationships and rebuilding trust. Some sins, like arrogance and pride, are a perverse desire for status and superiority. They can only be addressed by those willing to humble themselves before others."[88]

While there may be different remedies to various sins, according to the Law, the Bible says they can be atoned for by only one method: the atoning death of Christ. God has said, legally speaking, the consequence for sin is death, and the legal requirements can be met by the perpetrator or by an innocent substitute, so that mercy can legitimately be extended to the perpetrator under certain conditions as long as justice has been satisfied.

Jesus' death satisfies the legal requirements of God in that he represents all humanity, as did Adam (Romans 5.12-21). Adam was an archetype of the human race, and in his sin all humanity became separated from God. So also in Jesus, as an archetype of humanity, all can be redeemed by grace through faith as a result of His righteousness.

ACCUSATION: THE BIBLE SAYS SLAVERY IS OK, AND GOD ENDORSES SLAVERY.

Dr. Paul Wright, the president of Jerusalem University College, says,[89] "When we think of slavery, the first thing that comes to mind is either slavery in the pre-Civil War U.S. or slavery as we hear it in places of the modern Middle East (via ISIS or such groups).

"The textual evidence that we have for slavery in the ancient world (—by this I mean the ancient Near East, the context in which ancient Israel arose, not ancient Rome) shows by and large a different kind of 'institution' (that's not the right word to use). For this reason, the Hebrew word, *eved*, is better translated 'servant.' The overall textual evidence from the ancient Near East shows that slaves had certain rights—they could own property, for instance, or determine inheritance. Or they could become free, as the Bible allows, given certain circumstances. They were typically not bought and sold, opposite as the case in the

---

[88] David Brooks, The Road to Character (New York, NY: Random House, 2015)
[89] from an email from Dr. Wright

medieval and modern worlds. 'Forced Labor,' or the corvée, is a more complicated issue, essentially a tax on person by the government for a certain period of time (e.g., 1 Kings 9:15). Note that the servants that Israel is allowed to take from among the foreigners are able to receive inheritance from their "owner" (Lev. 25:46).

"The larger question is to what extent the Bible participates in the world of the ancient Near East, and to what extent it expresses a set of ethical standards which at the same time presuppose it yet works to change it. There's a whole lot of middle ground, actually. This is what makes an understanding of the context of that day so vitally important as a place to start."

Dr. Wright continues that "there is no evidence of chattel slavery[90] in the ancient Near East. While slavery was known in many cultures there, the type of slavery was debt-slavery, punishment for crime, enslavement of prisoners of war, child abandonment, and the birth of slave children to slaves."[91]

Even about Leviticus 25.46 ("You can will them to your children as inherited property and can make them slaves for life") Jacob Milgrom says: "The law merely indicates that the jubilee doesn't apply to non-Israelite slaves. 'It does not imply that the slave is a piece of property at the mercy of his master' (Mendelsohn 1962:388)."[92]

And lastly, there is absolutely no extrabiblical data on any slaves in Israel. The private and public documents of the ancient Near East from 3000 BC to the times of the New Testament are full of references to the practice of slavery in the parallel cultures, but nothing from Israel. Cole agrees and says that "slavery in Israel was rural, domestic, and small scale. There were no 'slave pens' of imperial Rome, or the racial subjugation of colonial America."[93] What seems likely is that slavery hardly existed in ancient Israel.

---

[90] **Chattel slaves** are individuals treated as complete property, to be bought and sold. **Chattel slavery** was supported and made legal by European governments and monarchs. This type of enslavement was practiced in European colonies, from the sixteenth century onwards.

[91] Paul Wright, *Rose Then and Now Bible Map Atlas* (Torrance, CA: Rose Publishing, 2008), p. 27

[92] Jacob Milgrom, Leviticus 23-27, The Anchor Bible Vol. 3B (New York, NY: Doubleday, 2001) p. 2230

[93] R. Alan Cole, Exodus (Downers Grove, IL: InterVarsity Press, 1973) p. 169

ACCUSATION: THE TRINITY IS A SELF-CONTRADICTION AND IS ILLOGICAL.

There are several ways that the Trinity is perfectly logical. The Trinity does not violate the law of non-contradiction, but there is a paradox. While some things seem to be self-contradictory, there are both possible and logical ways to reconcile the alleged variance. For instance, we know light exhibits the characteristics of a particle and of a wave. So while it is a single entity (substance), it manifests itself in various ways. It's a paradox, but also a reality.

Another way to look at the Trinity comes from an idea posed by Sheldon Vanauken in *A Severe Mercy*. His idea was this: Suppose I write a book, and I put myself in it. The character "me" says what I would say and does what I would do. It's ME in the book. He's exactly as I am. Now, is the character in the book different from the me outside of the book? Of course he is. But is it me? Of course it is. He's all me, but he's all a separate character. I can easily be both the author and a character without compromising either.

In addition, we know that some people view human beings as unified entities, that we have no soul or spirit, but we just *are*—all of me is all there is of me. Some people, however, view humans as bipartite—a body and a mind. Is that a contradiction, to think that the "mind" of me is somehow a separate entity of the "body" of me, and yet I am "me," a unified whole? Not at all. It's possible. It's difficult to know the truth and reality of such things, but it's both possible and possibly reasonable.

In the Bible, the Trinity distinguishes between the principle of divine action and the subject of divine action. The principle of all divine action is the one undivided divine essence, but the subject of divine action is either Father, Son, or Holy Spirit. The Father can send the Son according to his power, and the Son can be incarnated according to his nature without dividing the divine essence (as in the three analogies).[94]

---

[94] Kyle Claunch, *"What God Hath Done Together: Defending the Historic Doctrine of the Inseparable Operations of the Trinity,"* Journal of the Evangelical Theological Society 56/4 (Dec. 2013), pp. 797-798

[91] Rev. Dr. Joe Boot, "The Trinity and Social Justice," *Jubilee*, Spring 2015, pp. 8-9

Joe Boot also explains: If God is not a Trinity, love is not possible, because there is no "me" and "you" before the world was created. There is no diversity, no plurality, and no relationship. And if there was no relationship, then God needed us to be able to be "love." And if he needs us, he's not God. Without the trinity and therefore without diversity and plurality, there can be no foundation for knowledge, love, morality, or ethics. Indeed, without an absolute personality, there is no diversity or distinction basic to reality at all; ultimate reality is a bare unity about which nothing may be said. Moreover, because a denial of the Trinity leads to a denial of an absolute personality, we cannot speak coherently of the *will* of God. Only persons have a will. But if God has no will, then creation is not the free act of an absolute, personal God, making creation itself impossible.[91]

The Trinity is both a logical and necessary part of creation, love and life.

ACCUSATION: IF GOD KNOWS EVERYTHING, THERE IS NO SUCH THING AS FREE WILL

The accusation is if God knows everything that is going to happen, then we are predetermined, and if we are predetermined, there is no such thing as free will, and none of us is responsible for our actions or accountable for them.

To address the accusation, we must establish that our definition as "human" is dependent on free will. There are several facets to this.

First of all, the ability to reason is grounded in free will. Reasoning involves deciding if something is true or credible by equating it to the reality to which it refers, then comparing it with competing ideas, and choosing which idea best fits reality. Without free will and the legitimate ability to choose, the role of reason itself in any intellectual discipline is suspect—there is no mechanism for evaluating information and deciding on plausibility. Without free will, then, science itself is an illusion, all conversations are meaningless, and our thoughts are unreliable. Our lives are irredeemably incoherent.

We study our natural world (the sciences) as if self-awareness, self-direction, and reason are real. We can evaluate that there are realities outside of ourselves that we can observe and draw true conclusions about. The notion of truth takes us beyond mere biological determinism, which is only concerned with survival (food, flight, fight, and reproduction). We act as if we honestly believe that we can ask "what if..." questions, assess the possibilities, make authentic decisions, and conclude truth. All of these are evidences of free will, reason, and objective truth, all of which show that we live and function as if these things are real, reliable, and even have a facet to them that could be considered "true."

Secondarily, if free will didn't exist, we couldn't know it, because I can't evaluate possibilities or draw conclusions. I couldn't think my way out of a paper bag let alone ascertain free will. Without free will, we couldn't know anything. Knowledge is justified true belief. As I've already established, we decide if a belief is true by comparing it to the reality to which it refers, comparing it with competing ideas, and choosing which idea best fits reality. This requires some level of free will. If you don't believe in free will, then you don't believe in the validity of reasoning, and all arguments to the contrary are self-defeating.

Third, without free will, the characteristics that most make us human are impossible: love, forgiveness, grace, mercy, and kindness, to name a few. If I have no choice but to love you, it's not love at all. Love requires the will to choose. If the only reason I forgive you is because I have no other alternative, then I have not forgiven you at all, but only followed an irresistible force. Without free will, I am a determined animal, perhaps even robotic, but I am not human.

Fourth, without free will there is no such thing as justice. I can neither find nor enforce justice in a court of law if there is no self-direction, either on the criminal's part (he can't be held accountable if he was determined to do it) or on the judge's part (he can't make a rational decision if there is no such thing).

One cannot have free will without self-direction, and one cannot have self-direction without self-awareness, and one cannot have self-awareness without consciousness. The evidences are convincing that we have all these things. I have consciousness, therefore I am self-aware, and therefore I am self-directed. Both reason and experience tell us these things are so. Everything about humanity and reason point to the necessity of free will.

Now let's deal with the question of God's omniscience. That God knows everything has no impact on my freedom to choose. Knowledge has nothing to do with causality. No matter what I know, it doesn't make you do anything. Suppose I know you love chocolate, and I know every time we go for ice cream you pick chocolate. My knowledge has nothing to do with your choices, and doesn't cause you to do anything. It doesn't even matter what I know or how much I know. My knowledge, or anybody's knowledge, does not and cannot have any effect on your behavior. Knowledge doesn't *cause* anything outside of its own entity. It matters not whether it's trivial or substantial, because knowledge can only have an effect in someone or something else if it is linked with a power (a causal mechanism) to create an effect. Knowledge by itself is impotent as a causal mechanism in another entity. No matter how much I know, you can never say that my knowing something caused (forced) you to do something. Knowledge just doesn't work that way.

But suppose I'm twice as smart as I am in real life (wouldn't that be nice). How does that affect you? It doesn't. Suppose I'm ten times as smart. How does that affect you? It doesn't. Suppose I'm omniscient. How that affect you? It still doesn't. Knowledge is passive, not causal. Just because I know something is going to happen doesn't mean I caused it to happen.

ACCUSATION: CHRISTIANITY AND SCIENCE ARE NOT ONLY INCOMPATIBLE, BUT CONTRADICTORY.

The accusation is that science has proved Christianity to be false. It is said that what scientists have learned about the Big Bang and evolution makes Genesis laughable. And now that we know about science, it's easy to see that the alleged miracles of the Bible are just the foolish explanations of primitive and ignorant peoples. And since we know about science, all the inaccuracies of the Bible about the earth resting on pillars and the sun revolving around the earth make the Bible a thoroughly mythological and false work of writing.

These accusations are unfounded. We have spoken about the Big Bang in Chapter 1 of this book, and about evolution previously in this chapter, as well as miracles. No aspects of science or Christianity are automatically or necessarily at odds with each other. Rather, there is great agreement between the two. The Bible teaches that nature is orderly, predictable, beautiful, purposeful—all characteristics we see in nature. The Bible teaches that humans have meaning, value, reason, purpose, and a sense of right and wrong—all things that are compatible with what we observe in humans.

The scientific method requires that nature be orderly, regular, and predictable, that our ability as humans to reason is reliable, that we are capable of weighing alternatives and arriving at truth. Science requires that knowledge is possible, can be reliable, and that the external world is real. These are all completely compatible with Christianity.

Some would claim that science in general supports only a naturalistic position, and the concept of God is incompatible with this "scientific" worldview. But neither classical science nor quantum mechanics supports such a position. It is true only if science can prove by laboratory methods and scientific inquiry that the being of God is impossible. Yet such theological/philosophical conclusions are outside of the realm of scientific experimentation. On the contrary, scientific discoveries provide assertions that establish good foundations for the existence of God (purpose, design, regularity and order, reason, etc.).

"Modern Western empirical science originated and flourished in the bosom of Christian theism and originated nowhere else. It was Christian Europe that fostered, promoted, and nourished modern science. Modern science is a legacy of Christianity."[95]

"With respect to the laws of nature, therefore, there are at least three ways in which theism is hospitable to science and its success, three ways in which there is deep concord between theistic religion and science.

---

[95] Alvin Plantinga, Where the Conflict Really Lies (New York, NY: Oxford University Press, 2011) p. 266

1. Science requires regularity, predictability, and constancy; it requires that our world conform to laws of nature. From the point of view of naturalists, the fact that our world displays the sort of regularity and lawlike behavior necessary for science is a bit of enormous cosmic luck, a not-to-be-expected bit of serendipity. But regularity and lawlikeness obviously fit well with the thought that God is a rational person who has created our world and instituted the laws of nature.

2. Not only must our world in fact manifest regularity and law-like behavior: for science to flourish, scientists and others must *believe* that it does. Whitehead: 'There can be no living science unless there is a wide-spread instinctive conviction in the existence of an *order of things*.' Such a conviction fits well with the theistic doctrine of the image of God.

3. Theism enables us to understand the necessity or inevitableness or inviolability of natural law: this necessity is to be explained and understood in terms of the difference between divine power and the power of finite creatures. Again, from the point of view of the naturalist, the character of these laws is something of an enigma. What is this alleged necessity they display, weaker than logical necessity, but necessity nonetheless? What, if anything, explains the fact that these laws govern what happens? What reason if any is there for expecting them to continue to govern these phenomena? Theism provides a natural answer to these questions; naturalism stands mute before them."[96]

ACCUSATION: THE EXODUS NEVER HAPPENED, AND IT PROVES THE BIBLE IS FALSE.

We'll start off by discussing a basic question: What is it you're expecting an archaeologist to find?

---

[96] Ibid. p. 282

1. Most archaeological remains are found in the destruction layers of cities (tells). What would one expect to find of a people group on the move for 40 years, building no cities, subject to little military action, and taking all their possessions with them? We have to be realistic about what one expects to find as evidence. Mostly what an archaeologist might hope to find is skeletons, but since they would be scattered about, even that would be a challenge. The egalitarian nature of Israelite society, however (confirmed by excavations in Canaan during Joshua's era, when they know Israelites were present in the region), yields precious few artifacts, even skeletons of the dead. The Israelites buried in simple burials outside settlements, in open fields with no grave goods.

2. Archaeologists have to give some promise to secure money for their digs. There is very little money in digging about in the desert trying to find traces of a wandering people. Archaeologists dig on tells, primarily, because that's where the greatest prospect of finding objects and information of value is.

3. There are no surviving papyrus documents from Egypt's Delta. It's too wet. Papyrus is where most of the records were documented, except for the carvings on the inside of the tombs of the great achievements of the king. Devastating spiritual plagues and exodus are not the kind of things kings want to proclaim as their legacy for history to read. The inscriptions that are on statues and temple facades tend to be propagandistic. Where papyrus records have survived, they tend to be from desert areas. So we understandably have very few of the day-to-day court records of 3,000 years of Egyptian history.

4. The Bible implies that the Israelites lived among the Egyptians, not necessarily in a separated location (Exodus 3.22). They may not have left behind artifacts that are distinctively Israelite. If they lived with and among the Egyptians, the artifacts to be found just may be of an Egyptian character.

5.

6. The Nile delta has moved during the millennia. Possibly the evidence we're hunting for is somewhere out in the Mediterranean.

7. No one knows the exact location of Mt. Sinai, and archaeological remains are scarce in the Sinai Peninsula. There is in Midian, however, a "holy" mountain surrounded by literally *thousands* of artifacts and carvings relating to the time period and the situation of the Exodus.[97] Perhaps, as scholars are still evaluating, Moses led the people in their wanderings through Midian (a theory that would make sense given that he had spent 40 years there) rather than the Sinai Peninsula, and perhaps these abundant remains are exactly what people are looking for.

Secondly, the stories of a large population of foreigners working as slaves for the Egyptians accords well with everything we know about Egyptian culture during the mid-second millennium BC.

1. Archaeologists have uncovered the well-preserved village of Deir el-Medina, showing us conditions under which Egypt's own laborers worked, and it matches the conditions described prior to the Exodus. This village was inhabited for over 400 years.[98] The narrative of the Exodus is realistic to what history and archaeology have found.

2. We know from extrabiblical sources that immigrants habitually and regularly entered and settled in Egypt. Some are depicted in the tomb of Khnumhotep at Beni Hasan (1850 BC). The best known large-scale immigration involves a group of non-Egyptian Middle Easterners we know as the Hyksos who actually ruled Egypt, at least over the northeast Delta, as Dynasties XV & XVI (1650-1550 BC). This gives support for the realism of the Israelites being in Egypt prior to the Exodus.[95]

---

[97] Hershel Shanks, "Where is Mt. Sinai?," *Biblical Archaeology Review*, March/April 2014, pp. 30ff.

[98] Leonard & Barbara Lesko, "Pharaoh's Workers," *Biblical Archaeology Review*, Jan/Feb 1999, pp. 36-38

[95] Ibid., pp. 36-38

3. About 400 years after the Hyksos, Dynasty XIX came to power in Egypt, including Pharaoh Ramesses the Great. The 430-year Egyptian sojourn could have spanned the era from Hyksos to Ramesses. The Ramesside family originated in the NE Delta (where the Israelites are said to have lived) and came to the throne through the office of the vizierate, the pharaoh's prime minister and chief justice. The Ramessides certainly had some non-Egyptian roots, as indicated by the choice of the name Seti. The biblical account of Joseph, a Hebrew, in power in Egypt is a realistic portrayal of political personages in Egypt.[99]

4. In the 13th c. BC, during the reign of Ramesses the Great (a.k.a. Ramesses II), the old Hyksos capital of Avaris in the northeast Delta was rebuilt and expanded under the new name of Pi-Ramesses (Exodus 1.11). This could have been the work of Israelites, as the Bible mentions.

5. The place names of Ra'amses and Pithom in Egypt (Exodus 1.11) are in harmony with what we know of the Late Bronze Age, when there was extensive construction in the Nile delta region.

6. An Egyptian tomb discovered in the late 1980s in Sakkara, Egypt, contains the coffin of a Semite named Aper el along with the coffins of his wife and children. His titles include "vizier," "mayor of the city," "judge," "father of god," "child of the nursery." This tells us that a Semitic-speaking foreigner like Joseph, and later Moses, could have risen to the highest levels of Egyptian government.

7. James Hoffmeier points out that Aper el's name was the first of a high-ranking Semite official to be found there, even though Sakkara has been excavated and explored for more than a century. "If such a high ranking official as Vizier Aper el was completely unknown to modern scholarship until the late 1980s, despite the fact that he lived in one of the better documented periods of Egyptian history [14th century], and was buried in arguably the most excavated site in Egypt, it is wrong to demand, as some have, that direct

---

[99] Ibid., pp. 36-38

archaeological evidence for Joseph should be available if he were in fact a historical figure."[100] This is even more the case, he says, because Joseph lived during a period when surviving Egyptian documents of any kind are sparse and because Joseph operated in the Nile Delta, an area that remains underexcavated to this day.

8. The Tabernacle built by the Israelites is described as a portable prefabricated shrine. There are Egyptian parallels of similar design in the 2nd millennium BC. It could be evidence of the Israelite presence in Egypt. The ark of the covenant is also like a portable clothes chest found in the tomb of King Tut (1336-1327 BC). There is no reason to believe that such an artifact could not be manufactured by the Israelites, and it shows that they could have been under the artistic influence of Egyptians.

9. The accounts of the Exodus ring true to nomadic life: nomads living in the Nile delta were exploited for cheap labor, Moses' flight to Midian was a common escape route, Bedouins knew how to find water in the wilderness, even by striking certain rocks, matzah had origins in Bedouin life, etc. These give credibility to the narrative.

10. An Egyptian papyrus reveals a middle-eastern slave with a Biblical name identical to the name of a midwife mentioned in Exodus: Shiphrah (Exodus 1.15). It is reasonably certain that the papyrus came from Thebes. The point is not that this is the same woman, but that such names date to the era when Israelites were believed to have been in Egypt.

11. The Merneptah stele clearly shows that before the last quarter of the 13th century BC there existed an "Israel" as distinct from Egypt and outside of it, though there is a strong Egyptian presence in the land of Canaan.

12. The Wisdom of Merikare and the Prophecy of Neferti, ancient Egyptian documents, report influxes of thousands of Semites into the Nile Delta between 2200 and 2000 BC. Similar patterns of settlement recurred over the next

---

[100] Kevin Miller, "Did the Exodus Never Happen?", *Christianity Today,* September 7, 1998 Vol. 42, No. 10, Page 49

thousand years, creating a "significant Asiatic (Middle Eastern) population" in the Delta region. The Merikare document explains that these Asiatic, Semitic speaking peoples, like Jacob and his sons, had come to the fertile Delta area in search of food during times of famine.

13. There is abundant evidence in all eras that Egyptians were slave owners. Foreigners, captured in war, were enslaved. Pharaoh Thutmose III (1479-1425 BC) brought back almost 90,000 prisoners from his campaign in Canaan. All this supports the very real possibility of a large population of Israelites in Egypt.

14. In a surviving Egyptian document called Leiden Papyrus 348, orders are given to "distribute grain rations to the soldiers and to the 'Apiru who transport stones to the great pylon of Rames[s]es." This brings to mind Exodus 1:11, which says the Hebrews "built supply cities, Pithom and Rameses, for Pharaoh." While hotly debated, 'Apiru is believed by some scholars to refer to the Hebrews, the 'Ibri.[101]

The descriptions of the geography of Egyptian borders and fortresses are accurate to the era. Recent discoveries of military outposts on a road leading from Egypt into Canaan, built by Pharaoh Seti I and earlier kings in the 13th c. BC, shed new light on why a northern route for the Exodus would have meant war for the Israelites. Exodus 13:17 states: "When Pharaoh let the people go, God did not lead them by way of the land of the Philistines, although that was nearer; for God thought, 'If the people face war, they may change their minds and return to Egypt.' " Instead, the Bible explains, "God led the people by the roundabout way of the wilderness."[102] While it is virtually impossible 3,000 years later to retrace the footsteps of a people who escaped over a sand swept wilderness, an Egyptian letter (Anastasi III) from guards at a "border crossing" between Egypt and the Sinai helps explain Moses' insistent cry, "Let my people go!" The text indicates that in the 13th c. the Egyptians maintained a tight border control, allowing no one to pass without a permit. The letter describes two slaves who—in a striking parallel to the Israelite escape—flee

---

[101] Kevin D. Miller
[102] Kevin D. Miller

from the city of Ra'amesses at night, are pursued by soldiers, but disappear into the Sinai wilderness. "When my letter reaches you," writes the official to the border guard, "write to me about all that has happened to [them]. Who found their tracks? Which watch found their tracks? Write to me about all that has happened to them and how many people you send out after them." Another inscription from the same cache of documents (Anastasi VI) records that an entire tribe gained permission to enter Egypt from Edom in search of food.[103]

The lack of direct Egyptian evidence doesn't prove the Exodus didn't happen. Egyptian sources could have been indifferent to the Exodus and the takeover of Canaan.[104]

The point I am making is that everything about the possibility of an Israelite presence in Egypt, with one of them in power, and an escape route into the wilderness is historically and geographically plausible. There is nothing in the story told in the Bible that is questionable; there is no evidence against any written there. Research bears out that when Egyptologists write about connections between Egypt and the Old Testament, they have generally accepted the Bible's claims. In Nicolas Grimal's A History of Ancient Egypt, he says, "It is considered possible that the Jewish Exodus may have taken place during the reign of Ra'amesses II." He finds the lack of evidence for this event "not in itself surprising, given that the Egyptians had no reason to attach any importance to the Hebrews." Ronald Williams, another Egyptologist, said, "The evidence is overwhelming that Israel drank deeply at the wells of Egypt."

It is true, and it goes without saying, that there is no hard and direct evidence for Israel's presence in northern Egypt in the 2nd millennium BC, and there is no direct evidence for the event called the Exodus. The indirect and supporting evidence, however, is very plausible. Every element of the Bible story is compatible with what we know of the history and geography of the time. There is nothing in history or archaeology that has confirmed the Exodus story as untrue.

---

[103] Kevin D. Miller

[104] Abraham Malamat, "Let My People Go and Go and Go and Go," *Biblical Archaeology Review*, Jan/Feb 1998, pp. 62-66

CONCLUSIONS:

In the end, each of us must make inferences that lead us to the most reasonable conclusions. What I have tried to present in this book is that belief in the God of the Bible and in Jesus, His Son, is a reasonable pursuit, and carries with it a battery of evidence that is rational and convincing. Christians never need to make excuses for their convictions, nor be embarrassed about them. Belief in God makes sense of our world and in our world, and I find the evidence compelling and convincing.

1. YHWH's nature, as He has revealed Himself, conforms to our highest reasoning in theology and philosophy: all-knowing, all-powerful (without self-contradiction), completely other (transcendent) and yet completely engaged (immanent), loving but just, judging but merciful, maintaining standards and yet full of grace, never-changing but flexible to human situations, communicative, eternal, creator, able to work wonders, and yet without going outside of His nature. This is the God of the Bible. As far as Jesus, God in the flesh, we see a person of compassion, power, and kindness (who doesn't take guff from detractors). If God were here in the flesh, we would expect him to be fearless, relational, with words of authority and truth, a knowledge of people and situations, and a complete knowledge of the past and future. We would think God in the flesh would be sacrificial and not self-oriented, full of patience but not a pushover, meek but not a doormat, assertive, humble, and yet confident. This is exactly what we see in the biblical record.

2. The Bible presents a world that we see. As opposed to other religions, it presents a world where evil is real and where God lets things take their course but intervenes to keep his plan of redemption on track. It portrays humanity as noble but hopelessly lost, moral but corruptible, both good and evil, torn between self and others, having a conscience, knowing purpose, aware of morality, acknowledging beauty,

capable of creativity, but in some ways also animalistic and capable of horrific behavior.

3. The Bible portrays "religion" not as a way to earn a place in God's graces, but as God reaching out to us, to love his way into our hearts. This theology corresponds to reality because if we have to earn our way, we are all in hopeless trouble. But if God would just reach out to us, invite us into the kingdom, pay any sacrifices himself, and make a way for us to find him, come to him, and be redeemed, this makes sense as the only possible way someone could ever find salvation, and this is what the Bible teaches.

4. A true religion must engage the whole of the human nature, not just the mind and not just the emotions. It can't possibly just be about swaying to the music, entranced and brainless, caught up in the rhythms, spells, notions and potions. By the same token, it can't possibly just be about deep philosophy, debating the intricacies of theology, connecting intellectually with the mysteries of the universe and transcending humanity to enter the divine. True religion engages the mind and can fulfill the most intellectual queries, but at the same time enjoys expression, joy, uplifting emotions and the pull of our hearts. True religion is for the scholar and the child, the patrician and the plebeian, the civilized and the barbarian, the slave and the free, the man and the woman, the scientist and the poet. Christianity conforms to these categories.

5. A true religion must make sense out of history. It doesn't function above it or without it, compete against it or necessarily endorse it. Christianity is a historical religion where God works in and through history, accomplishing His purposes, involved in people's lives, bringing about the redemption of all creation.

6. A true religion must make sense out of science. It doesn't function above it or without it, compete against it or necessarily endorse it. Christianity teaches principles of cause and effect, beauty, regularity, predictability, purpose, design, reason, and a world in which science is possible.

7. Christianity teaches purpose, significance in humanity, forgiveness for wrongs, life out of death, hope for the hopeless, redemption, fairness, love, beauty, a God who is there, knowledge, conscience, renewal, and meaning.

I haven't even mentioned such things as the beauty, power, and authority of the Bible, the resurrection of Jesus, and the life changes that Christianity brings to so many.

Here's the true scenario: God created the cosmos as an adequate place for him to live, and to be a place that reflects his nature. (No man-made place or thing could even come close.) In a desire to share his love with even more beings than the Persons of the Trinity, God created humans in his image and likeness so that he could enjoy an honest relationship of love with each and every one. As we all know, love that is forced isn't love, but must be freely chosen and freely acted upon. God shared his love with humans, he shared his creation, he shared some of his character traits, and he designed a place, the earth, where He and humans could have this relationship of love with one another.

Astoundingly, people used their free will for selfishness and followed a desire that took them away from God, separated themselves from Him, and their minds became darkened. Our actions didn't reduce God's love for us, though, and he initiated a plan to get us back and to restore the broken relationship. Knowing that we could not save ourselves, God has made every provision for our rescue, offering it as a free gift to all comers. We must repudiate what separates us from God (repent of our sins), and turn to him in love (very different from "religion"; it's much like a marriage ceremony, where you forsake all others to commit yourself in love to the one who loves you.) But since love still must always be chosen and never forced, he informs and invites all people to come to him for rescue (salvation). The choice is each individual's, and always ours. No worthiness is involved, but only choice and love. All sincere comers will be accepted. All who refuse and choose to have nothing to do with God will endure the consequences of that decision: life without God, and eternity without God, if they get all the way to the end of life spurning his every invitation.

For those who choose to love God and devote their lives to him (again, much like a marriage), He offers forgiveness full and free, no matter what a person has done. That person's sins are cleansed, and he is justified—made spiritually whole, and the relationship with God is restored. Jesus spiritually comes to live inside that individual in the person of the Holy Spirit, little by little remaking that person to be like God. The individual works out his or her salvation by doing his or her part in conforming to the image of Jesus, and God does His part in a work that's called sanctification.

This conforms to everything we know about the world. The cosmos is an amazing place, reflecting wonders still greater than our powers of observation. Humanity has an almost inexplicable nobility, but also a staggering cruelty. We can easily see that what the Bible says about humans being in the image of God but fallen by our own poor choices is comprehensible. The Bible says we have purpose, significance, a conscience, meaning in life, a sense of beauty, a propensity to glorify self, a stunning curiosity and intellectual capacity, and a knack for both glory and stupidity. The Bible says this life is not all there is, but there is more to this life than living and dying.

If this writing work has been convincing, you must know that anyone can turn to God at any time. All you need to do is turn to God in prayer, repent of your sins, express your desire to love God, and give your life to him. It's both the easiest and the hardest thing you'll ever do, but ultimately the most right decision anyone could ever make. The choice is yours.

For Further Reading:

Jeffrey Burton Russell, Exposing Myths About Christianity
Paul Copan, Is God a Moral Monster?

55247729R00080

Made in the USA
Charleston, SC
23 April 2016